MW01106438

MARINE

featuring: The Battle of Hickory May 1967

Dr. Philip E. Ayers

xulon PRESS

Marine
featuring: The Battle of Hickory May 1967
by Dr. Philip E. Ayers

Printed in the United States of America

ISBN 9781624195570

Unless otherwise indicated, Bible quotations are taken from NKJ. Copyright © 1982 by Broadman & Holman Publishers.

www.xulonpress.com

Table of Contents

This book is dedicated to all combat veterans. It is especially dedicated to the Marines of the 2nd Battalion 26th Marines with the 3rd Marine Division who fought in Vietnam. It is a testimony to their bravery and honor shown on the battlefield.

This book is written in memory and gratefulness for the Marines who were wounded and especially those Marines who died in Vietnam in the Battle of Hickory in May 1967. They are the true heroes.

This book is a work of appreciation devoted to the families of all fallen Marines! I thank you for your great sacrifice in giving your sons, daughters and grandchildren to preservation of freedom!

I am especially grateful to Billy Mitchell who helped me authenticate the actions of this battle. He was a great man, historian, and Marine!

Semper Fi!

Endorsements

O peration Hickory was one of the bloodiest and worst battles that occurred during Vietnam. For some reason there are only a few lines devoted to it in history other than Mark Cauble's book, *"Into the DMZ,"* which is a battle history of Operation Hickory.

I have just read Philip Ayers manuscript on the Battle of Hickory and can say without a doubt that this is a correct rendition of the battle. My machine gun team was attached to his squad and we were involved in almost all of the events that he relates.

This is what occurs in the Marine Corps infantry during battle, though much of it is hard to believe by the ordinary citizen. It did happen. These true stories will keep alive the memories of the true heroes, the ones who died and did not come back. It will also record in history what they did and sacrificed for their country and fellow man. As Colonial Duncan D. Chaplin III USMC (Ret) said about the Marines of 2/26: "These warriors indeed earned the Red Badge of Courage in the history of warfare."

This story shows the true meaning of Semper Fi (Always Faithful). We had men who were wounded and did not want to leave our unit unless they were forced to. Some examples are: Second Lieutenant Robert Brown, Corporal Philip Ayers, Corporeal Lyons and Lance Corporal Joe Bannister.

I feel that we upheld the long traditions of the USMC with pride, just as the Marines today are doing in battle. This is a real story of the real Marine Corps: The Infantry in battle during war time.

> Billy Mitchell
> Marine Corps Vietnam Veteran
> M-60 Machine Gunner, Gulf
> Company, 2/26

The vivid description of the personal battles of Operation Hickory brought back memories of the sights, sounds and smells of the vicious battles that took place in the DMZ during May 1967. I have had these memories locked deep in my head for so many years. Dr. Phil, job well done!

> Jerry Dallape
> Marine Corps Vietnam Veteran
> Guns 1st Squad 1st Platoon
> Foxtrot Company, 2/26

Readers follow the unique experiences of an ex-Marine who becomes a pastor. The author reveals how turning to God has healed his Post-Traumatic Stress Disorder, guilt and restructures his ideas of death. This story of faith and courage is sure to capture audiences, as they understand the importance of accepting Christ as their savior.

Manuscript Review by Xulon Press

Dr. Phil Ayers has written an accurate account of the Vietnam horrors of battle. His account of my unit taking Hill 117 brought back terrible memories of those days. Many brave men died and were wounded in that battle. I received two Purple Hearts. I want to thank him for his willingness to share our story!

Roy Kessinger

Marine Corps Vietnam Veteran

Hotel Company, 2nd Platoon, 2/26

M-60 Machine Gunner

Congratulations on your book! I have read it and cried. Thank you for helping fellow Marines face their inner soul and realize that all of their efforts in Vietnam are appreciated. I have given your book to my children to read and have written notes on some of the pages. I am getting comments back from them and disbeliefs of what really was happening there. I finally realized the exact day that I received my 1st Purple Heart on May 18th during the mortar attack. My best friend Dennis was also wounded and evacuated along with the lady French reporter. They were taken out on an Ontos to a Medevac area. I was wounded (shrapnel in my head) but stayed there with you and continued on until the end of the campaign. I then had to have the shrapnel removed because of infection. I transferred out of "Galloping Gulf" in July of '67 and joined the CAG program living in the villages between Phu Bai and Hue. SF

Charlie Sichmeller

3rd Platoon, 2/26

Commander VFW

Junker-Ball Post 1865

Kenosha, Wisconsin

Phil Ayers is a Marine I trained at Parris Island. He had been in Vietnam longer than me, and when I arrived in Vietnam he was in the 1st Platoon of 'Gulf' Company, 2nd Battalion 26th Marines. I was assigned as Platoon Sergeant of the 2nd Platoon, but when we lost the Platoon Commander of the 3rd Platoon I took his job until we got more officers. Later I became the Platoon Sergeant for the 3rd Platoon. It was during this time that one of our companies had numerous causalities while encountering an NVA regiment. 'Gulf' Company, 2nd Battalion 26th Marines, moved up to reinforce them, and in the process took heavy casualties also. I got hit with shrapnel in my left ankle, our company's Supply Sergeant was shot through his knee and our Executive Officer was shot in his neck. The Corpsmen were getting all the wounded of our Company into one area.

In the meantime, the NVA were still in some of their fighting holes behind the 1st and 2nd Platoons. They were hindering the evacuation of our wounded. We needed to evacuate our wounded, so I ordered an Ontos to move forward and rescue them. While this was going on I was hopping around offering help to our wounded. A Marine from the 1st Platoon of our Company came up to our group of wounded and told me Corporal Ayers was hit with white phosphorous. When they brought up Corporal Ayers, his head was all wrapped up and also one of his hands. I was concerned about his eyes thinking he will be blind the rest of his life, if he even survived. I couldn't get out of my head that I was the one who helped train him and what I could have done better.

> Benjamin L. Leith,
> First Sergeant USMC (Retired)
> Marine Corps Vietnam Veteran
> Gulf Company, 3rd Platoon, 2/26

Forward

𝒫hil Ayers is a great friend of mine, but he is more than a friend. Phil Ayers was my student at Liberty University when he was working for his Doctor's Degree, and he was an outstanding student. He pastors one of the churches in Liberty Baptist Fellowship, and has done an outstanding job for 31 years. He is a golfing buddy of mine and he always beats me in golf in every area - distance driving, chipping and putting. Another great thing about Phil is his loyalty to the United States and the Marine Corp in which he served. Read the commendation from the US Navy for Phil Ayers.

On October 3, 1967, Colonial F.J. Gilhuly awarded Sergeant Philip E. Ayers the Navy Commendation Metal for service as set forth in the following citation: "For heroic achievement while serving as a squad leader with Company "G", 2nd Battalion, 26th Marines with the 3rd Marine Division in connection with operations against the enemy in the Republic of Vietnam. On May 17, 1967, during Operation Prairie IV near Phu Oc in Quang Tri Province, Corporal Ayers' Squad which was maneuvering to a position on his platoon's right flank, came under intense mortar fire and immediately sustained numerous causalities.

Quickly evaluating the situation, he skillfully deployed the remainder of his squad to covered positions and then repeatedly moved across the fire-swept terrain to administer aid to the wounded and assist in their evaluation. Returning to his squad through the heavy enemy mortar fire, he continued to direct and prepare his unit to continue its attack against the enemy. His exceptional professionalism and bold initiative were an inspiration to all who observed him and contributed significantly to the accomplishment of his unit's mission. By his courage, outstanding leadership and selfless devotion to duty at great personal risk, Corporal Ayers upheld the finest traditions of the Marine Corps and the United States Naval Service. Corporal Ayers is authorized to wear the Combat "V". He was meritoriously promoted to sergeant.

Even if you are not much of a reader, this story can change your life. Some of you may not have lived when America was fighting the war in Viet Nam. When you read about Phil's bravery, you will understand more about Phil Ayers. I read this book and it is very gripping.

Read the whole story, not just the glory and gore of the Viet Nam war, read his journey from being a high school dropout to becoming a decorated US Marine. Phil's courage and faithfulness to duty, projects the greatness of America's military men and women who have fought wars all over the world, but it's more than America's military that is important to him. Phil Ayers reflects the heart and soul of a true American. We love our nation, we will do anything for our nation, even die for our nation.

Phil Ayers is the pastor of Glade Creek Baptist Church in the small town of Blue Ridge, Virginia, about halfway between Lynchburg and Roanoke, Virginia. In addition to pastoring the church, he teaches at Virginia

Western Community College and services his community in many self-sacrificial ways.

Elmer L. Towns

Co-Founder and Vice President,

Liberty University

Preface

This story of my experience as a Marine and a combat veteran in Vietnam has a purpose. It is to remind future generations, those who come behind us, about the history and truth of the fighting men and women who voluntarily sacrificed their time, talent and life for freedom. It specifically tells the accounts of the 2nd Battalion 26th Marines of the 3rd Marine Division during the Battle of Hickory in May 1967. These experiences can be verified by the Military Chronology of Classified Records of Battle, the original First Platoon Diary, the testimonies of Marines, who were there, the book *"Into the DMZ"* by Mark A. Cauble, and my personal diary.

There are many historical accounts written about the conquest for Con Thien and "Leatherneck Square." I have written my account in a novel format with a personal intimacy for I believe this approach will bring to light the true grit, bravery and personality of men in combat. I have always felt the best way to learn of an event is through the eyes of one of its participants. Therefore I am exposing a time in my life that is personal and true. My story, however, might very well be a portrait of many other Marines who also served. The photographs are those of the Marine Corps archives, and the collections of Billy Mitchell, Bob Brown, Jerry Dallape and Phil Ayers.

The events and people referenced are true and the photos contained in the book are actual pictures taken during the battle. My wife was the first to read this manuscript. She said, "Philip, people aren't going to believe this! It seems impossible what you men faced. You were just kids."

The accounts of battle that you are about to read may seem unbelievable, but combat is that way, unbelievable. The power of prayer can also be unbelievable, yet, you will see evidence of the influence of prayer throughout this story. Prayer works!

Americans are free today because of the unselfish sacrifice of the dreams and lives of men and women on a battlefield somewhere far away from home. These warriors were exceptional in the performance of their duty with honor. Their unbelievable bravery, as well as their obedience to their oath to defend and protect this great nation is keeping us free. Their shed blood on the fields of Vietnam, in the trenches of World War I, on the hallowed ground of Europe and the Pacific Islands, on the ice-frozen reservoirs of Korea and the deserts of the Middle East have provided you and me the privilege to express our rights as citizens of the United States of America. In World War I, 320,710 veterans were wounded and 53,513 killed. In World War II 1,078,162 veterans were wounded and 292,131 killed. In Korea 136,935 veterans were wounded and 33,651 killed. In Vietnam, 211,471 veterans were wounded and 47,369 killed. We must never forget them!

There are no individuals who would desire to be killed. I do not believe heroes are born, but they are men and women who have no other choice than to respond to their circumstances in heroic acts of bravery. Keni Thomas, a Navy Seal and a squad leader in the rescue mission in Somalia, in what has become known as "Black Hawk Down", summarizes these warriors. He said no one would choose to fight and die on the battlefield. But when a warrior is put in a position to step up for freedom and his fellow comrades, heroes are made and valor is common place. There is not just one great generation to celebrate in this country, that of World War II, there are many.

The 2nd Battalion 26th Marines of the 3rd Marine Division was part of a great fighting force with a rich tradition. The 3rd Marine Division earned its reputation in the Battle of Iwo Jima in World War II. Its reputation as a fighting force continued in Vietnam. It landed in Vietnam on May 6, 1965, at Da Nang and quickly became involved in some of the heaviest fighting of the war. It was used in and around "Leather Neck Square" in the DMZ Theater. Battles, such as Con Thien, Gio Linh, Cam Lo and Dong Ha, helped win the Presidential Unit Citation for the Division.

The Marines of the 3rd Marine Division killed 8,000 North Vietnamese Army (NVA) soldiers during this period. My unit, 2nd Battalion 26th Marines (2/26), was part of this action. The 3rd Marine Division, between 1967 and 1968, had 1400 killed and over 9000 wounded. Five Metal of Honors and 40 Navy Crosses were given to courageous Marines during this period. They are the ones who were chosen to be decorated. Every Marine fought with honor, courage and pride. I know because I was there and I saw the acts of valor by Marines who could have been awarded the same metals!

1

Ours Is A Great Generation

Phil Ayers – LU graduation

I sat in the vast coliseum at Liberty University watching my oldest grandson graduate from high school. I studied each graduate as they walked across the stage to receive their diplomas, each and every one different in their own way. Each one has different futures and plans; some will continue their education and some will go into the work force. Still others like my son, Philip, Jr., and grandson, Jordan, choose to have careers in the United States Army. I felt immense pride watching Jordan receive his degree and I laughed when he cut up as he walked across the stage. They looked so young to me. I thought to myself, "Did I look that young so many years ago?"

I found my mind drifting back to 1965, to my youth although mine are not pleasant memories. I quickly lost the innocence of my youth, as did hundreds of young people of my generation. We were kids, eighteen and nineteen-years-old, asked to perform duties that should only be appointed to men. My generation faced the enemies of freedom in Vietnam and my grandson will face today's enemies of our nation. My generation served an ungrateful nation, full of division and hostility, but Jordan will serve a nation that is proud of our armed forces fight against terrorism. There is one common thread that exists between all generations of the fighting men and women of America; we serve with dignity and demonstrate bravery with honor!

This book is about my personal experience as a Marine, but it is far more than an account of my experiences in the United States Marine Corps. This book tells what makes a Marine — from civilian life to combat engagements. It demonstrates the individual and team perception of self-preservation and confidence instilled in the training and proven record of combat readiness of the Marine Corps. It is about every Marine that put on the uniform. We are comrades and our stories mirror one another. We are a brotherhood that never ends not even in death on this Earth. Our memories continue throughout eternity; once a Marine, always a Marine. I say to every Marine who fought with 2nd Battalion 26th Marines, this is about you. Your story of how you arrived in Vietnam is different than mine. The courage, honor and pride with which you fought as part of the 3rd Marine Division are ours together. I say to you, "Semper Fi!"

Much has been said, and rightfully so, about the "Greatest Generation". Author Tom Brokaw wrote a book about that generation. It was a best seller for many months in America. I believe in my heart there is another great generation, and it followed that one. It is the next generation that followed those of World War II.

I intend to tell you one small account of those brave members who, in days past, represented our great nation. It is true that our service did not involve the saving of a world from tyranny but it just as well could have. The fighting and dying for a cause was as great or more so. In World War II, each Marine spent an average of 40 days in actual combat. In Viet Nam each Marine spent 142 days in combat. The Marines who fought in Vietnam saw their buddies die, be mutilated and bleed to death in their arms. They saw the life go out of their comrades' bodies, and this left their minds wounded for life. The acts of heroisms are uncountable. These acts happened as a daily regularity. Every wounded and killed veteran was a person with dreams and hopes and family. All are heroes. We, the generation of Vietnam fighters, belong to that theater of glory!

2

Taking A New Direction In My Life

✠

I have found that life has its defining moments; snapshots of times gone by that bring joy or sadness to one's life. Some people only have one major incident in their life that forever changes the direction of their life. They are the fortunate ones. Most of us have many defining moments. I happen to be one of those people. The entire story of a person's life, if they were to tell it, would fill volumes of books. I am interested in sharing only those parts of my life that may help others face their defining moments. I have come to realize that you cannot delete a snapshot of past events, but you can embrace them and heal by the grace of God.

My story starts in October of 1963. I was in the locker room of Andrew Lewis High School. My teammates and I had just finished a gruesome football practice. I was about to take a shower when someone yelled to me to come outside. Someone wanted to talk to me. I said, "Can it wait?" They replied with great urgency in their voice, "No." I put my pants on and stepped outside into the evening coolness. There outside of the locker room was Vivian, my neighbor. I will never forget the expression on her face. It was one of dread, panic and deep hurt. She did not have to say anything. I knew something had happened to my mother. I was able to make out a phrase between her sobbing, "Your mother has had an accident! We need to go home."

Phil Ayers – ALHS football

I ran back into the locker room and grabbed my shirt and shoes. By the time I returned outside she had gone to her car and was ready to go. I got in and sat silently. She drove straight to my house. Nothing was said between us. Mike, my younger brother, and several of the neighbors were standing on the porch. He was crying and they were trying to console him. I rushed by them and went inside. I did not see my mom or my father at first. I found him in the kitchen talking with the police. "I heard him say, "I have no idea why she would do such a thing!" I wondered what they were talking about. What had mom done that would cause the police to come to our house? Had she gone to the country? It was obvious she was not in the house. I had looked for her as soon as I entered the house. About that time, Vivian had caught up to me and asked to speak to me alone. She was still crying. I think I knew, then, what she about to tell me. I had an empty, dead feeling deep inside me. We went into my bedroom, and she told me my mother was dead. I would learn later she had been hit by a Norfolk and Western train. Her words were like a lightning bolt hitting me. They burned my heart. It appeared she had committed suicide. It was not until years later that we realized that was probably not the case.

I raced out of the room, out of the house and down the street. I am sure someone must have tried to stop me but I was numb to any voices or surroundings. We lived in West Salem on Wildwood Road. It was nearly five miles from town. I just walked and thought. No tears. No speaking — just thoughts bombarding my mind. It was my worst nightmare. "Why had this happened? What was I thinking about leaving her alone?" I thought, "I should have stayed with her." I knew she was upset. She had several breakdowns, and had undergone shock therapy. I remembered her sitting at the kitchen window and crying for hours, and my helplessness to do anything about it. Nothing I said helped but I wondered if I could have said something this morning. I felt rage swelling up within me. I was already angry with the world and my inability to make things right at home. I felt as if she was my only lifeline, and now she was gone. I thought she loved Mike and me and now she was gone!

My mind went back to that morning and the talk we had. She was worried about my anger. It was so out of control and as usual it caused us to fight. She wanted Mike and me to leave the area and go with her to her brother's farm. It was in the fall of the year and in the middle of football season, so I refused to go. I told her, "Do whatever you want because that's what you will do anyway." I scolded myself, "How stupid of me to say such a thing." I remember her standing at the front door as I boarded the school bus. She had a look on her face that I cannot explain, but I felt in my heart that I would never see her alive again. That image is forever frozen in my mind. I wanted to get off the bus to say, "I love you", but I did not. I felt she had hurt me, so I was determined to hurt her. I wanted to scream but I couldn't!

I must have been in a daze because I nearly stepped in front of a car. The sound of the horn brought me back to reality. I had walked all the way to town and was about to cross the street in front of my girl-friend's house. Barbara, my girlfriend, had been the only help for me for a long time. She, and especially, her mother, unknowing to me at the time would save my life. They were my safe haven!

I first saw Barbara at Andrew Lewis High School. She was coming out of her English class on the second floor. I nearly passed out. She looked exactly like Hayley Mills, the teenage movie star. I was your typical fifteen-year-old boy with a mad crush on Hayley. I had it bad for her. I was asked to leave the movie house once for staying through five showings. It was not hard to fall head-over-heals in love with Barbara. Or at least what a fifteen-year-older felt was love. I followed her, at a distance, to her next class. I figured that way I would know some of her routine. I asked around and found out her name and that she was not dating anyone. It was not hard for me to acquire information since I was a football player and kids were more than willing to please us.

Barbara was a very pretty girl. I loved everything about her — the way she walked, dressed, talked and smiled. She brightened my day by just being there. I finally built the courage to ask her out on a date. It was a great surprise to me that she said, "Yes." We would double date with friends and did the things young kids did back then — drive-in movies, walks, bowling. She became a good friend. It was through her that I met her father and mother.

They were special people, not anything like my parents. They were God fearing people and very devout Methodists. They were the first to really take an interest in my view of God, which wasn't much. My father was an alcoholic, and he lived for the weekends so he could carouse with his drinking buddies. My mom lived in fear of what he might say or do when he was drunk, and so did Mike and I.

I envied Barbara's home life. I never told her, but I longed to be around her house. Her mother replaced my mom, and now looking back on things, I believe that hurt my chances with Barbara over the long haul. I can't blame her for pulling away from me. After all, who wants a brother for a boyfriend? Don't get the wrong picture. We were steadies for a while, nearly a year. And deep down in my heart, I knew she cared a great deal for me. Together, we endured the assassination of President John F. Kennedy and the invasion of the Beatles. She accepted my moods and jealousy. She was one-of-a-kind, and she was there for me when mom died.

I knocked on her door that evening. Hazel, her mom, came to the door. I did not have to say why I was there. She had heard the news on TV. I can't really remember a whole lot of that night except that they stayed up with me through the night. Barbara was allowed to stay up, and we sat on the couch in their living room. She held me. Her parents were sitting across the room. We didn't say much, as I remember. What was there to say at a time like that? I will forever be in her debt for understanding the moment. The next day her dad, Durwood, took me home. It was the first time I rode in his station wagon — a story for another time. That was a privilege.

I was not met with a welcome. Mike was still asleep, and Dad was sitting in the kitchen in a daze. Arlene, his friend, was holding his hand. I remember wanting to kill both of them. We didn't speak. I went to my room and fell asleep. When I awakened she was gone and didn't re-appear until days later. It was probably a good thing that she didn't.

The next few days were a daze for me. It was like I was in a fog, and everyone around me were strangers. I hated going to Oakey's Funeral Home in Salem to the wake. I never understood why people would call a place that harbored dead people a home. I would really hate walking by the place after school on the way to Barbara's house. It was on College Avenue, which was the way to her house from Andrew Lewis High School. It kept the wounds fresh.

The wake was awful, as you might imagine. Everyone was crying and clinging to each other. People were speaking with my father and acting as though he was an innocent party to the whole affair. I wanted to vomit. Mom's casket was closed which I thought was strange at first. I had been to my dad's brother's funeral and his coffin was open so everyone could see him. I was sickened when I overheard someone talking about what a mess mom's body was after being dragged so far under a train. I hurried into another room and tried to dismiss the thought from my mind. That one statement made me have nightmares for months to come about how she must have looked. I suppose I should have cried at that moment, but instead I fought back the tears and hardened my stature. It is a snapshot I have not been able to delete from my memories.

The day of the funeral was horrible, people wanting to hug us and give their condolences. I know they meant well but sometimes people just need to shut up. Sobbing could be heard throughout the chapel as the preacher spoke about having faith in God and eternal life. I thought to myself, "What a joke!" My mom's family was there — Aunt Virginia and Uncle Walt with their kids Brenda and Karen; Uncle Villie and his wife, Edith with their kids, Hebron, Martha and Dianne; Aunt Othie and her husband, Ralph, with their kids, Mary, David and Allen Lane. It was obvious that they were hurting. After all, they had lost a sister. I am not sure who else was there but I am sure everyone was present. I remember them because they were sitting closer to me. They are a close family.

Death became a reality to me at the graveside when we sat down with mom's casket before us. I knew she was gone forever, and I would never hear her voice again or feel her embrace. She would never watch me play another football game or help me with my homework. I would never see her waiting for me to come home after school or have her ask me about my day. I would never taste her cooking, smell her beans simmering on the stove or see her smile again. I made some decisions at that moment. You never know what is going through the minds of people at funerals, but I committed to never go to funerals or funeral homes again. The preacher finished his speech, and everyone started to mingle. It was so awkward. I just wanted to be with Barbara and her folks. Hazel said it would be alright if I wanted to come to their house that afternoon.

I tried to stay to myself but no one seemed to think that was a good idea. They kept approaching me and wanting to say something profound. Maybe someone had something good to say but I didn't hear it. I was too numbed. One person tried to counsel me to let my emotions out. "It is alright to cry," she said. I replied in a harsh way, "Why? It is a sign of weakness and is for fools!" as I turned and walked away. Everyone went back to our house after the burial but I didn't stay long. I went to see Barbara.

Months went by and things continued to escalate. Football season was back again. My friends didn't know what to say, and the teachers acted like I had the plague. I suppose they were afraid I might ask them a question that they were not ready to answer. I acted on the outside as if nothing had happened but on the inside I was changing. My anger was building until it exploded one day in football practice when I unloaded on our quarterback as he was attempting to run a play. I hurt him and angered the coaches. They sent me to the locker room, and my day was over.

Things continued to worsen. I couldn't focus on my responsibilities for my position on the football team. I would forget the plays, and that cost the team. I was expelled from a game for kicking an opponent while he was on the ground. Finally, I was benched. Barbara and my relationship had just about run its course. She was avoiding me even though I was still spending much of my time talking to her mom. I got into a fist fight with one of the neighbor kids and hurt him severely. My grades were falling. I was a mess!

My home life was no better since Arlene was spending more and more time at the house. She didn't like Mike and me, and the feelings were mutual. I spent as much time as possible away from the house, but the problem was that Mike had no place to go. He was stuck, and I regret not being more sensitive to his feelings and needs. He paid a higher price than I did by being around the masquerade at home. His is

15

another story and only he can tell it. If I was not in Salem visiting Hazel, I was with my best friend Steve Brown, but I was hardly ever at home.

Football season passed and nothing great happened in my playing. It was a mediocre season for me. My team-mates kept to themselves, and they left me alone to live in my own anger. Spring was around the corner. Just over a year had passed since mom's death. Basketball season came and went. Now, it was baseball season, and I had earned a starting position on varsity as a catcher.

Coach Joyce, who was also the head football coach, had taken a special interest in me. In fact, he moved me into the catcher's position in the place of their last year's starter. It was a mixed bag of feelings for me. On one hand, I was excited to be starting, and on the other hand it didn't really seem to be that great, maybe because Barbara and I were not getting along. My grades were continuing to fall, and I knew that if I didn't bring them up, I would be cut from the baseball team. My nightmares continued to keep me awake at night. It was a sad time. I hoped when the baseball games started things would improve but they didn't!

It was game day, and I was excited for school to start for a change. I dressed that morning in the best clothes I could find that were clean. I was not the best keeper of house chores, such as washing and ironing clothes. The athletes at Andrew Lewis had to wear a coat and tie to classes on game day. I ironed a shirt, and I had a tie, but the problem was I didn't have a good pair of dress shoes to wear so I wore cowboy boots. They were black and not offensive in appearance. Or at least, I didn't think they were. I polished them and went to school.

I was leaving Algebra class when I heard my name called, "Phil Ayers." I turned to see who wanted me and it was Mr. Barnett, our Assistant Principal. He was furious over my cowboy boots. He believed I was trying to mock the school policy. I tried to explain, while we headed for the office, that they were all I had that was decent to wear. He would have nothing to do with my explanation. I still think he remembered an argument we had several weeks earlier. My attitude was not good at the time. Nonetheless, he called the principle to come to his office.

It didn't take long before they decided to expel me for three days. School regulations were unrelenting on school officials at the time. They were in the process of explaining I would receive all zeros for my classes for those days and that my parents would have to sign me back into school. I said, "Parent." "Don't be smart with me!" Just as I was about to answer, Coach Joyce cleared the door to their office. Someone had told him what was happening. He almost tore the hinges off the door entering the room. He reminded them that my mother had passed away. There was silence for a moment. I was asked to leave the room and close the door behind me.

I am not sure what was said, but I could only hear parts of what was being said. But Coach Joyce and Barnett had a temper so you might imagine the scene. They were nose to nose at times. Soon Coach Joyce opened the door and asked me to come into the office. He said, "I would have to leave for the three days but that. . ." I interrupted him and said I would fail the grade with zeros. Before anything else was said, I turned and walked out of the office and out of Andrew Lewis, only to return six months later. Mr. Barnett and Coach Joyce, without knowing it, shaped my life and helped me become the man I am today. They were good men.

Now, I had a real problem since my father had told me that if I failed school I either had to go to work or go into the military. And I was sure this would totally end a relationship with Barbara. I remember being so angry and so empty. I felt undone. I was frightened and confused as to what would happen next. It is a wonder that I didn't end up in jail or worse. I decided to wait to tell my father about what had happened until I turned seventeen in a few days. I had no way of knowing that my life was about to change forever!

Over the next few days I spent countless hours talking to Hazel, and she had such good advice. I should have listened to her. She wanted me to go back to school and was willing to go with me to school and speak on my behalf. I think she truly loved me and would have taken on the entire school board for me, but I would have nothing to do with that idea. My pride had been stepped on and I had made my decision to join the military.

3

Leaving Home

$\mathcal{I}$ remember the day I took the local transit bus from Salem to Roanoke. It was three o'clock in the afternoon. It cost me thirty-five cents one way. The recruiters were located on Campbell Avenue across from the Roanoke Court House. I was lonely that day. I cannot really explain my feelings. I know I was somewhat afraid of the thought of leaving town. It took some time for the bus to go from Salem to Roanoke, so I had some time to think. I thought I wanted to join the Air Force. I had always liked to fly and had flown in Hilton's bi-plane several times. He owned a local flying service at the airport in Roanoke. My next door neighbor, Paul, would take me with him a few times a year when he was taking pilot lessons.

The thought of joining the Air Force ended when I walked through the door of the recruiter station and saw a Marine recruiter standing in the hall dressed in his Dress Blues. He was a tall, rigid looking man and his countenance was stern, demanding respect. I immediately knew

I wanted to wear that uniform! Really I had no choice since the other military branches were not taking seventeen-year-olds at that time. But it would not have made a difference. It was the Marine Corps for me!

He must have seen the sparkle in my eyes as He motioned for me to come to his cubicle. We sat down and he asked, "What brings you here today?" I really didn't know what to say to him. My eyes were fixated on that uniform. He continued, "Do you want to wear the uniform? I replied, "I sure do!" He continued with his questions, "Are you in school?" To which I answered, "No." "Are you in trouble?" "Sort of", I answered. "I was suspended from school and my father says I have to go to work or join the military." His face stiffened, "Are you in trouble with the law?" I quickly said, "No!"

The next few minutes were spent with me telling him my story, but He did not seem to be very impressed with it. It seemed to mirror most of the boys going into the Marines. Finally, he stopped me and asked, "What do you like? Do you like shooting or hunting? Can you fire a rifle?" Boastfully, I replied, "I can shoot a penny off a rail fence at 100 yards any time I want too!" He laughed. "That good, are you?" I sprang to my feet and spun around to leave. No way was I going to be made fun of. I had had enough of that to last me a life-time. He stopped me in my tracks. "Sit down young man!" His voice was demanding and somewhat frightening. He had my attention, and I sat back down.

He pulled out a large packet of forms from his files while saying, "We can use you. How old are you?" I answered, "Seventeen." He continued, "Will your parents sign for you to join the Marines?" "My mother is dead but my father will be more than happy to get rid of me." "Good!" I don't remember all the information he shared from that point. I simply signed my name where he pointed to on the forms. He asked, "When can I meet with your father?" He needs to sign a few papers also." I said, "Any time after five. He gets off work at four and is usually home by then." "How about tonight?" "That's good." We stood up and he shook my hand. I will never forget that hand-shake, firm and to the point. I would shake hands the same way from that moment on with everyone I met.

I looked at my watch as I stepped outside onto the sidewalk. It was nearly five o'clock and the last bus back to Salem left at five. I ran down the street and around the corner to the bus stop. Several people were already standing there so I knew I had not missed it. The bus came, and we boarded and headed to Salem. My thoughts were running wild. I could see myself in those Dress Blues and people respecting me. But, also, I was fearful. I had never left Salem and Roanoke except to go Floyd to my uncle's farm. Sure, I had been to Ohio once to see my mom's sister but that was when I was a kid and mom and dad were with me. Now I was about to leave Virginia and go to a place called Parris Island in South Carolina. Was I sure I wanted to do this? I wavered back and forth more times than I can remember on that ride to Salem. One thing was for sure. The recruiter would be at the house soon. I hurried from the bus stop to the house even though I was not sure what to say or do. My father's car was parked in the driveway so I knew he was home.

He was in the living room reading the newspaper when I walked in and sat down across from him. "Dad, I have made a decision." "Oh, what is that?" He didn't even look up from reading the Roanoke Times. "I am joining the Marine Corps." "When?" "Tonight, if you will sign for me. The recruiter is coming tonight so you can talk with him and ask him any questions." He acted as if he hadn't heard me for a few minutes. He looked up from the paper and asked, "Are you sure?" I said, "Yes", and that was the end of the conversation. It was about as short as the talk we had when I told him I was expelled from school.

I went to my room. Mike was there and he was crying. He had heard my talk with dad and was upset. He was just a kid, and I was not very sensitive to his feelings. In fact, I wasn't sensitive to him at all which I regret because it left him to fend for himself. I think I tried to explain to him that I had no choice but I'm not really sure. It seems like something I should have done. Whether I did or not I can't say for a fact. I do remember my leaving home broke his heart! I know now, as I look back on things, I should have stayed at home, not only for his sake but for a lot of reasons. Life was going to change for many people very soon.

It was not very long before the recruiter was knocking on the door. It was about seven o'clock. I was waiting and saw him pull up in his car. It was Marine Corp green. There was no missing the emblem on the door, the globe and anchor with the eagle perched on top with its outstretched wings. He was very imposing in his demeanor and very much about his mission of signing me up. My father entered the room, and they shook hands. I couldn't help but notice the difference in each of these men. The Marine was proud and regimented while my father was humble and appeared to be like a mouse about to be eaten by a cat. I must say it didn't take very long, about five minutes to sign everything. It was kind of funny in a way because I had to re-sign the forms I had signed earlier. I signed my name with two "L's", not knowing my name only had one "L" in Philip. My father had no questions and the recruiter wasn't interested in staying around to talk. I do remember him saying to my father that the Marine Corps would make his son a complete man, physically, mentally and spiritually. He told me he would call me in a few days with my orders to go to Richmond to be sworn in.

The next morning I walked to Barbara's house. She was at school but Hazel was there. She was always there. What a great mom and friend she was to us. She asked what I had been up to lately, and I told her I had joined the Marines and was awaiting a call to leave for boot camp. She was visibly shaken by my news. I think she knew what was ahead of me and feared for my health and safety, but she didn't share those feelings with me. She was too wise to do that. Instead, she said she was proud of me and that she would always be praying for me. Coming from her that meant a lot to me. We sat there and drank coffee together. She had her cigarette, and it was a calming time for me. I felt at peace in her presence.

The time flew by. Barbara came home later than usual from school. I knew I needed to tell her I had joined the Marines so I asked her for a few minutes of her time. She was in a hurry, and I think she was annoyed that I was there, yet again. Our relationship was strained, and I think she was interested in someone else. Nevertheless, she was somewhat moved when I told her. She hugged me for some time and told me she was sorry things were the way they were. I appreciated that because I knew she really did care about me. Durwood was coming in the door from work so our embrace ended more quickly than I had wished. Hazel invited me to stay for supper. Durwood and I talked for a very long time. Barbara went out with some friends and I left for home just before dark. I remember it was a cold March evening and an unusually long walk home. I felt like I, at least, had a future but the uncertainty of it all was depressing. I remember being very sad that night.

Several weeks passed until it was time to leave for boot camp. It was April 1 — April Fool's Day. My visits with Hazel were many and very rewarding. I felt I had a purpose for going into the service. I would be fighting for our country and good people like Durwood and Hazel, Barbara, Mike, Steve and his folks. I cannot remember for the life of me how I got to the Greyhound bus station in downtown Roanoke that day. It's a blur to me, but I do remember being alone. I had said my goodbyes the night before. It was emotional for Hazel. My father was out until everyone had gone to bed so I didn't say goodbye to him. Mike was quiet. He didn't cry but I could see he was hurting. It was hard to leave him. I suppose I should have hugged him and said more than I probably did, but I was immature and hardnosed, none of the males in our family hugged each other. Hugging other males was seen as a sign of weakness and there was no way I would show any kind of weakness to anyone. He was still asleep when I left the house the next morning. I have often wondered what he felt when he awoke, and I was already gone.

It was exciting to start my new life. The ride to Richmond was beautiful, as I remember it. Virginia was a beautiful state, and I was getting to see it in style; well, at least from a bus window. The ride took several hours but soon we arrived at the Capitol Building. There were several of us going to Parris Island from Roanoke. There were more than twenty leaving Richmond to go there.

I will never forget taking the oath to defend our nation. Everyone who had joined was asked to repeat the oath after the commanding officer. Individually, we took our oath. "I, Philip Ayers, do solemnly swear that I will support and defend the Constitution of the United States against all enemies, foreign and domestic; that I will bear true faith and allegiance to the same; and that I will obey the orders of the President of the United States and the orders of the officers appointed over me, according to regulations and the Uniform Code of Military Justice. So help me God." It was the first time in a long time that I came close to tearing up. Very moving!

4

From A Civilian To A Marine – Becoming Physically Fit

The next day we boarded a train headed for Parris Island. This was my first train ride, and I was lucky enough to get a window seat. It was amazing to see the changing countryside. The mountains I loved so much became a distance feature on the horizon and soon disappeared. They gave way to flatland and tobacco farms. Then, cotton farms began to appear. The plants were not mature, but you could tell they were cotton plants. Just before dark fell, the land started to appear marshy. It was strange because the trees had an unfamiliar looking vine growing in them. I learned later it was a southern moss draping the limbs and touching the ground in some places. I thought to myself, "I am sure glad I live in the mountains." Then, it dawned on me that thought was no longer true.

I fell asleep only to be awakened by the conductor announcing that all enlistees were to embark at the next stop, Beauford, South Carolina. My heart skipped a beat. "How could we be there already?" Soon the train slowed to a stop and a drill instructor, known affectionately as a D.I., sprang through the door of the coach screaming to the top of his lungs, "You low life stupid fools. . . get to your feet and line up . . . now!" He was physical with us, grabbing and shoving us closer together. We were so close to each other that I could smell the hair of the guy in front of me. "Move, move, move!" he shouted. Everyone was stumbling over each other's feet trying to get off the train.

Once outside, he placed us in ranks. Four, I believe, and hurried us to a nearby barracks. One of the recruits made the mistake of saying something, nothing important, but enough to tick this D.I. off. That resulted in us going back outside, in the dark, picking up cigarette butts off the driveway. We did that all night long with him constantly yelling like a madman. There were always butts to pick up since he would scatter the ones we had picked up, over and over again. He never slowed down, and his voice never weakened! We were so tired. You may not believe it but even this was preparing us for those sleepless nights during combat.

We were glad to see an olive colored military bus pull up just after sunrise. I didn't think I could hold my eyes open any longer but I was wrong. The bus had four more drill instructors on board. These D.I.'s would be our worst nightmare for the next sixteen weeks. "Lord, help us", I thought. If you think the one was bad, just imagine four! They nearly knocked each other down clearing the door of the bus. They were on us like flies on honey, screaming, "Get on the bus, get on the bus, move it, move it!"

One stayed at the door of the bus. He was a big black D.I., Sergeant C.V. Edwards. He was in everyone's face, cussing each one of us and pushing us up the steps into the bus. I am not sure how many of us were there but the bus was full. We sat down and every seat was filled. My heart was racing, and I was actually trembling with the energy rush all of this was causing. It was not the picture the recruiter had painted for me back in Roanoke.

Staff Sergeant B. M. Nail and Sergeant B. Leith were suddenly standing in the isle way of the bus having a major fit. "Get up off your butts, you maggots. Get up, get up, get up!" Sergeant Leith was screaming to the top of his voice, "I dare you worthless pigs to sit without my permission." He acted like a madman.

Then, the head DI, Staff Sergeant Al Stafford, boarded and started his speech. "You maggots are our responsibilities for the next sixteen weeks." "Maggot" would become our affectionate name. He continued, "Whether you live or die is up to us. Today is April 13, 1965. You will never forget this day as long as you live. It is my job to see to that. These next weeks will be hell on earth and if you make it through them, you might be Marine quality. There is one way onto this island and one way off, across the Horse Island Bridge in front on us. Many have tried to escape Parris Island by way of the swamp. The alligators enjoyed them. You are not to speak unless we speak to you first, and you are to address us as 'Sir'. That means all we want to hear is 'Yes Sir or No Sir'. You will not have contact with anyone outside of this island without our permission, and that will not happen. That means you can only have mail and that's it. We will be your mama and daddy for the next sixteen weeks. Do you understand what I am telling you?" Without any hesitation we all sheepishly replied, "Yes Sir." They shouted, "What did you say!" We came back with, "Yes Sir!" They screamed the louder, "We can't hear you!" Suddenly we were screaming, "Yes sir!" Stafford told us to sit down, which we gladly did. The silence seemed deadly!

The bus pulled away, and we headed for that bridge. I remember thinking, "Do I have what it takes to be a Marine?" This was nothing like I had imagined. I felt like maybe I had made a big mistake. Suddenly, all the pleas that Hazel and some others had made to me rang more clearly in my ears. "Don't do this!" My thoughts were interrupted by the bus stopping. We were ordered off the bus and put into a platoon formation for the first time.

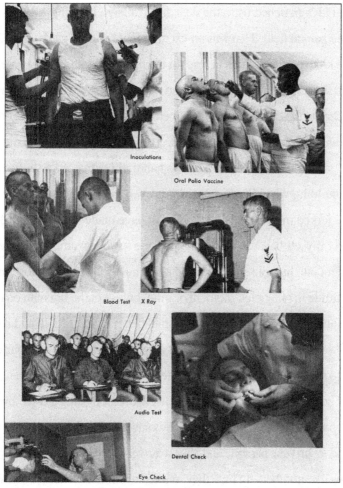

Parris Island

That was quite a task to endure. The D.I.'s lined us up by our heights. Since I was a scrawny 168-pound, six-foot three-inch kid, I was put as the first person in what was to be become the First Squad. Three other tall kids, Greg Drought, Alan Davenport and Ron Medley, were picked as the other squad leaders, and the other recruits were placed in the ranks behind us by their height, from the tallest to the shortest. We were now Platoon 222 of the 2nd Recruit Training Battalion.

The D.I.'s marched us to the next area, a large building, which was just across the parade field. That was an exciting few hundred yards. Imagine seventy-five kids trying to march in step for the first time with, what seemed to be, mad men screaming in your face that you were out of step, whatever that meant. We marched to the building, and then, lined up in single file to enter the doorway.

It was during this time that I realized I was not the celebrated figure of high school fame. I was leaning on the handrail leading up a short step way into the building when Sergeant Edwards eyed me. Before I knew what happened he jerked me off the handrail. I must have made a move toward him in defense of myself because he backhanded me to the pavement. I looked up in amazement into his cold steel eyes and knew not to say a word. I lost my entire smart attitude in one quick moment of time. I was not the big man on campus at this place. I knew I was nobody and had better fit their mold and real fast.

We were herded into a building in single file where we lost our dignity. We had to strip to our underwear and side step through a series of events which included being weighed, our heart beat checked, blood being drawn, and inoculated for polio. They took our civilian items and discarded them in the trash box.

I was a private person, and this was very embarrassing for me. They treated us like numbers. In fact, they marked a number on our chest according to when we were seen by the first medic. We were issued our utilities, 'skivvies', boots and socks, and our bucket called "782" gear. This gear, an array of straps, belts, buckles and poles would be used during the next weeks. And all of our hair was cut off, to the skin. It reminded me of the cow barns back home when we would herd the cows in one end of the barn, milk them and herd them out the other end. It was a shocking first day ending with us in our barracks, our pride destroyed, and dead tired.

Early in our training we were measured for our dress uniforms and our pictures were taken. We were given a series of tests to determine where we would serve once boot camp was finished. Strength tests were given before training started, and the number of push-ups, sit-ups and pull-ups we could do was recorded and tracked throughout our advancement through training. We were issued "dog tags". Our rifles were issued to us. The condition of our rifle was recorded at the time of issue, and we were responsible for it during training. My rifle would later save my bacon.

The first day of official training started with a bang. Or I should say with a trash can. Sergeant Edwards awoke us by throwing the trash can down the center isle of our barracks. He ordered everyone out of the bed (racks) and to attention in front of our own rack. We were instructed that every morning we would dress in our utilities, blouse (shirt), later to become a white tee shirt as hot weather approached, and boots. We would take our sheets off our rack and hold them out in front of us for inspection. I realized later that was done in order to weed out chronic bed wetters. Then we would run to the center of the squad bay with our dirty sheets, drop it in a pile and retrieve new ones and run back to our rack. We would then make our rack in military fashion, upon command from the D.I. in charge, and return to attention in front of our rack. Trust me when I say you never wanted to be the last one to come to attention. We would then, upon command, race outside, fall into our squad position forming our platoon and go for our morning run, which was numerous times around the parade field. The run would finish in front of the Mess Hall and breakfast. This would be our wake up routine for the next sixteen weeks.

31

Platoon 222

The first week was learning how to march and close order drill. This constant drilling developed teamwork and the ability to instantly respond to commands. We learned the commands of formation movement: Come to Attention, Parade Rest, Forward March, Reverse March, Column Right and Left, Eyes Right, Present Arms and Double Time. That meant running in unison by a cadence call. This was a sing-song routine that was shouted by the D.I. and repeated by us. We spent hours practicing these drills. They became second nature to us.

Not much can equal the sound of a hardcore Marine Corps cadence led by a thunderous D.I. and repeated in unison by a group of motivated Marines. If you've heard it, you know exactly what I'm talking about. If you've never heard it, words cannot describe the tingle it puts in your spine. If you're not sure if you've heard it, then you haven't. It is something you will never forget.

Most Marines' first exposure to this impressive display is from their D.I.'s during boot camp. The D.I.'s chant is loud and forceful about all matter of things. The chant mostly has to do with the guile, ferocity, and the fighting spirit of Marines, present, past, and future. Some involve verses you can take home to mom, and some are meant only for the Marine's ear. But regardless of their content, they all have the purpose of motivating a formation of Marines, keeping them all in step and breathing consistently, and pushing their endurance beyond the normal limits of any individual.

I still can hear my favorite cadence on those many morning runs, shouted first by the D.I. and then by us, seventy-five Marines strong. First the D.I. would shout the line, and then we would echo his call, one line at a time. "You can keep your Army khaki; you can keep your Navy blue. I have the world's best fighting man, to introduce to you. His uniform is different, the best you've ever seen. The Germans called him 'Devil Dog', his real name is 'Marine.' He was born on Parris Island, the place where God forgot. The sand is eighteen inches deep, the sun is blazing hot. He gets up every morning, before the rising sun. He'll run a hundred miles and more, before the day is done. He's deadly with a rifle, a bayonet made of steel. He took the Warrior's calling card; he's mastered how to kill. And when he gets to Heaven, St. Peter he will tell, one more Marine reporting, sir, I've spent my time in Hell. So listen, all you young girls, to what I have to say, go find yourself a young Marine, to love you every day. He'll hug you and he'll kiss you, and treat you like a queen. There is no better Fighting Man, the United States Marine!"

The morning routine was no problem for me. I had no trouble running since I was an athlete and could run as long they wanted to run. I did have one very potentially deadly event. We were not allowed out of our racks during the night, once lights were out. There were no excuses accepted for being

33

up, not even going to the 'head.' The civilians call it a rest room. One night I really needed to use the "head" but I knew better, so I tried to stay awake so no mistakes would happen. Instead, I fell asleep and wet the bed, not severely but enough to cause panic. I remember holding the sheet off the mattress in hopes it would dry through the remaining night. Morning came, and I was first to strip my rack. I held the sheet so no signs of my mistake could be seen unless the D.I. chose me to inspect. He didn't, and I flew to the center of the squad bay to throw down my sheet and retrieve a new one. That mistake never happened again! The rest of the day was easy compared to that possible disaster! Slowly but surely I was being transformed from a civilian into a disciplined individual that would follow any command of war.

Surviving the trip to the Mess Hall was a learned exercise. We always double timed to it in formation. We went everywhere in formation. The platoon was dismissed by squads, one squad at a time until every recruit was standing in the chow line. The squad with the most achievements went first. Then the others by order of their squad rank would join the line. It was important to be in the outstanding squad of the day because it afforded a longer time to eat. I thought the food was good especially after not having a regular diet for several years back home. I grew from 168 pounds to 190 pounds by graduation day, and it was all muscle.

The length of time to side-step through the chow line, get your portion of chow and eat it was determined by when the D.I. finished his meal and headed outside. The second he headed for the door everyone dashed to the galley and the plate return counter, and then, raced outside to fall in. Everyone had to be at the "at ease position" before the D.I. reached the formation. He would call us to attention and we would go to our next physical training or learning exercise. This routine never changed and it was the same for each meal.

Our regular routine for the day was regimented, as you would expect. The first exercise after breakfast was P.T. which was intense and punishing. I had been to Coach Joyce's summer football camps, and I thought those were the worst exercise and conditioning programs possible until I experienced the boot camp program. It was designed to turn our civilian flesh into Marine muscle and it did just that! We did push-ups, pull-ups, side straddle hops, sit-ups and up in arms with our rifles until we felt our muscles crying out in pain. By the way, for you who aren't aware of the exercise "up in arms", it is repetitions of raising your rifle from your waist to over your head. Each was one repetition. We would do 200 repetitions at a time. Then, we would do the push-ups. You should try this sometime. It will test your fortitude, especially when a D.I. is standing over you screaming how pitiful you are.

Obstacle course

35

The next event of the day was the Obstacle Course. It consisted of running a course designed to build your stamina or kill you. You had to go over and under parallel bars ranging from four foot off the ground to eight feet off the ground, and then, climb atop a ten-foot wall dropping to the other side. You had to jump long pits of mud and water. The finish was the most demanding. You had to climb a fifty foot rope to a narrow top beam, cross over the top beam, run a twenty foot narrow beam to the slide for life rope and slide down the rope by laying on it using your foot to balance yourself until you reached the ground. The course ended with a sprint to the finish line.

Once a week, on Sunday afternoon, we would compete, in field meets, with other platoons in different challenges — push-ups, sit-ups, pull-ups, fifty-yard dashes, running relays and disassembling and assembling weapons relays. We would dress in red athletic shorts and yellow tops. We had a very competitive platoon with some very good athletes and I was one of them. I felt like I found some favor with the D.I.'s during this training and I loved the challenge. It was kind of like being home. Of course, the D.I.'s never praised you but you could sense their true feelings of approval.

The entire platoon, as part of this exercise, would compete in a tug-of-war against the opposing platoons. I especially liked the tug-of-war game because it allowed us to win as a team. Some of the tug-of-wars would last for a long time with each platoon locked in a standoff, not able to move the other an inch. Naturally, our D.I.'s would encourage their favorites to put more energy into it. All of this training ended in our having to pass the PRT test at the end of the boot camp. This was a true test of our physical conditioning. It was like a game to me.

Another great team competition was the log carry. This log seemed to weigh a ton; it was about fifty pounds per man. The object was to pick it up and move it 100 yards from a starting line to a finish line. But before that took place, we had to do arm curls with it. Sometimes, depending on the D.I. in charge, we would curl it until we could not move. Then, the D.I.'s fun began. I swear these guys were half crazy with their expectations of us, and what is worst, we started to meet their expectations. The more they pushed the more we excelled.

The spirit of competition was high. I was very thankful for the stronger recruits beside me because arm strength was my weakness. They covered for me even though I am not sure if they realized it, but they always saved my bacon. Everyone wanted to please the D.I.'s. It seemed they held a spell over us. On one hand, we hated them, yet we loved them. I suppose you would have had to be there to understand. Anyway, the entire exercise ended up in a mad log carrying dash to the finish line.

Each day, also, consisted of indoor and outdoor classes. The indoor classes included fire arm maintenance where we learned to disassemble and assemble weapons, the .45 caliber pistol and M-14 rifle. We learned their nomenclature and how to properly clean each one. The D.I.'s spent long hours stressing the importance of military tactics and Marine history. They instructed how to pack a field pack, shine your boots and shoes, and personal hygiene in combat situations. These lessons would prove vital in the years to come.

In the afternoon, we were back on the parade field marching and practicing for the drill competitions that would come later. These close-order drills were difficult. We learned to go from rifles at attention to shoulder our rifles, go from the right shoulder to the left and to present arms. Presenting arms is especially difficult while marching in a straight line. The D.I.'s were demanding during this time. They wanted us to be perfect. It was their mission to win the Battalion Commander's Trophy which was a combat boot enshrined on a plaque. Every platoon sergeant wanted to win it and Staff Sergeant Stafford was no different. He acted as if he was demon possessed. He even jumped the other D.I.'s when we messed up. The hard training would pay off as we won the boot trophy in the competition. Team competition was vital. It would be no different in combat. Every Marine pulls together.

The weeks seemed to crawl by with each week's training becoming more and more difficult. It was extremely difficult for me to learn hand-to-hand combat. That always puzzled me because of all the altercations I had with guys back home. I think it was because we had to learn the Marine way of fighting, plus I never had intended to really hurt someone in those fights back home, but now I was being taught to kill the person in front of me. I never realized that I valued life until then. The truth be told, I didn't realize what dying meant.

The instructor was a special trainer, not one of our regular D.I.'s. He explained, "This training will teach you to develop confidence in your fighting skills. These skills are essential to your survival in combat situations. What you learn and practice now may mean the difference between life and death in combat." Then he asked for a volunteer. No one dared to move. Everyone stood frozen in place. Panic struck me when Sergeant Edwards picked me out of the group. "This hero will be your guinea pig", he snorted. He never had forgotten the first day and our misunderstanding of my intentions.

The instructor moved in real close to me. "Ever been in a fight with someone?" I replied, "Yes Sir!" "Did you win that fight?" "Yes sir!" "Can you beat me?" I hesitated for a second. A thousand thoughts flooded my head. I'll be smart this time I thought to myself. "No sir!", but that was the wrong answer. The next thing I remember was being face down on the deck (mat), his knee in my back and my head being pulled back to point of snapping my neck. He motioned for me to get up. While I was doing that he emphasized the need to never think you will lose a fight. He said, "It is sure death!" Those words brought a chill to my skin. He asked, "Would you like another chance at me?" Again, what was I to say? I gambled and said, "Yes sir!" "Right answer! You learn quickly," he replied. "Fall back in with your unit."

The rest of that session was spent in one-on-one fighting exercises. I learned I knew nothing of how to fight in a life-and-death circumstance until that day. We learned the kill zones on the human body and many different take-down techniques. The instructor was emphatic about never leaving your feet in combat with someone who is trying to kill you. This would prove to be a lifesaving lesson in Vietnam.

In the coming weeks we would see our platoon become a well disciplined unit. Esprit de Corps was developing, and it would be needed because the training was about to step up another notch. Remember the obstacle course. It seemed easy at the time but now we were facing another course, the confidence course. It appeared very opposing the first time I saw it. The set up was similar to the earlier one but with greater obstacles and more chances to fail or be hurt. Combat is like that, one obstacle after another.

Once again it started in a straight line with different obstacles spread out along the course. We would sprint twenty-five yards to the first obstacle, which was a series of logs mounted on a structure that suspended them about five feet in the air and spaced about five feet apart. The objective was to cross these ten logs without falling off.

The next confidence builder was the log climb. It was a ladder, made of logs that stood straight up and down with ten logs spaced three feet apart. We would climb up one side and down the other. From there we would run twenty-five yards to a large ditch which was traversed by swinging across on a rope that was hanging from a log tripod structure. The only way across was to run and jump from a ledge, grasping the rope that suspended from the tripod so that your momentum would allow you to drop to the other side.

The next hurdle was the rope climb to a platform fifty feet high, traverse across the platform to the other side and climb another twenty-five foot log ladder to another rope which we used to repel down to the ground, leading to the last challenge. It was to run to the next structure, which was another rope exercise. We had to climb the rope fifty feet to the top of a narrow platform, lay down on another rope that stretched from the platform to the ground. This rope was over water. We had to swing down under the rope and descend hand over hand. I remember my arms and legs felt like noodles by the time I reached this obstacle. If we fell off along the way, we started over from the very beginning. The course accomplished its purpose. I felt I could conquer anything after that. It was the hardest physical training to that day.

The most difficult and humiliating training of all was the combat swimming drills. This training consisted of two stages and took place two thirds of the way through the sixteen week camp. The swimming test was not a great challenge. It reminded me of the Boy Scouts summer camp and swimming to the diving platform in the middle of the lake at Camp Powhatan. All we had to do was demonstrate we could swim by swimming back and forth across the pool ten times, which was no problem. However, the next stage nearly sent me home.

The completion of stage two required that we jump off of the fifty foot high platform into the pool fully dressed in combat utilities, packs, and boots with a dummy M-14 rifle hanging from our neck. We were instructed that this simulated going overboard off a sinking landing vessel. Marines are amphibious and each man must be at home in the water as well as on dry ground. I jumped off the platform and hit the water off balance. Somehow I took in water and choked. In my panic I did not gather the air in my blouse as we were taught to do. This would make a primitive floatation device. So I didn't float and I sank back to the bottom of the pool. I desperately pushed myself upward and barely reached the surface, just enough to get some air. I sank again, just to repeat my effort to survive. That was bad because I had to stay afloat for twenty minutes while treading water in order to pass the test.

The instructors pulled me out of the pool after I went down the third time. I thought I would drown there in that pool. It was very humiliating and all the other recruits saw what was happening. The instructors revived me and put me back into the pool. I was allowed to get back into the water and keep moving for the twenty minutes needed to pass the test, but the damage had been done. I had no pride and I had let my fellow recruits down. I was removed from my squad leader's position and made to march thirty paces behind the platoon for the next week. I had to eat alone, and was not allowed mail call. I did push-ups while everyone else enjoyed reading their mail. The D.I.'s totally forgot my contribution to the platoon in the sporting events on Sunday afternoons, but later, I would redeem myself at the rifle range.

Things were not always so tough. Sundays were different. We had the field meets that I described to you. We were given time to wash our clothes using our buckets and a clothes line. Washing clothes, besides being a tradition in the Marine Corps, is an important part of recruit training. Clean clothes, neatly pressed, make a healthier and sharper recruit. My mind would wonder back to seeing mom hanging our clothes on her clothes line. I thought about what she would think of me now. Would she be proud of me? Sunday was the day for me to write home. The time was more peaceful and I could get my thoughts more organized. The other days of the week were survival days, but the D.I.'s seemed to give us a reprieve on Sunday.

Sunday also meant we went to church. We were marched to church where we heard different sermons, mostly on patriotism and God. We would sing hymns and take communion. The chaplain reminded me of Reverend Johnson from First United Methodist Church back home in Salem. Reverend Johnson was a kind and gracious man, and his sermons always made sense at the time, but I never did practice his instructions. After all, I only attended church so I could date Barbara. Her father insisted on that practice.

Church service on Parris Island was a time I longed for each week. It allowed for the God part of the motto, "God and country", to make sense to me. The D.I.'s were constantly yelling, "God and country maggot, God and country! We fight for God and country." I treasured this thought because I always considered myself to be a patriot. I loved studying about the history of our nation and especially the battles of the "War Between the States". It is hard for me to explain, but I felt a connection with those fighters of freedom, and now, I had a chance to be part of our nation's tradition of fighting men. I would be a Marine!

I remember standing at the Union's position on top of Cemetery Ridge at Gettysburg. Cemetery Ridge was a fitting name for a position that would claim 6,555 men of the Confederacy, killed or wounded in one charge. I was thirteen and visiting the battlefield on a school trip. I had a sense of pride, being a Southerner, as I looked across that vast field where Pickett's Brigade would charge the Union soldiers. I wondered how and why those Confederate soldiers would face the murderous fire of the Union Army. It meant certain death, yet they still charged across that open field knowing it meant they might be killed. It puzzled me greatly. "Would I do such a thing? Would I have the courage to face certain death for a cause I believed in so greatly?" Unknowing to me at the time, but the answer would come in May 1967, in the killing fields of the North Vietnamese Army in the Battle of Hickory.

We also had "free time", about an hour, at the end of each training day. We were allowed to take a shower and shave. We could pull our footlocker out in front of our racks and write letters or "spit and polish" our boots. This was the time we received mail from home. We could not talk to each other, however. This was not allowed. It was not a social hour and we had to stay to ourselves.

It was also a humorous time for some recruits. I am reminded of Private Drought. He was always in trouble with the D.I's. We were not allowed to receive personal mail that contained anything other than letters, such as chewing gum. The letters were to never smell of perfume. His letters always had both. I think his girlfriend was trying to kill him.

The D.I.'s would go nuts over his stuff. They would call him to the center of the squad bay and give him hell over this. I bet he did a thousand side-straddle-hops and push-ups for his mail over the sixteen weeks we spent there, but he never said a word, just did what they commanded of him. If that's not love, I don't what is.

Finally, I could see the end in sight. The sixteen weeks were nearing their end. The training intensified even more than ever, and it included close-in fighting which meant learning to bayonet fight. The bayonet and its use are a vital part of the Marine's combat training and goes all the way back to World War I. Speed, balance, timing, and above all, aggressiveness make the bayonet fighter. We were taught the basic stances and moves in bayonet combat fighting. The "pugil stick" fights proved whether we had learned the skills effectively.

A "pugil stick" is a stick with padding on each end of it, used in the place of a rifle to practice bayonet combat. Each recruit had to fight another recruit using these sticks until one of them was beaten into submission. It was demanding training, but absolutely necessary. Part of this training consisted of an obstacle course that had punching bags suspended from poles. There were ten bags spaced ten yards apart. The recruit had to run to each, stab the bag with his bayonet attached to his rifle, pull it out and run to the next bag until he finished the course.

Just before marching out to the rifle range we tried on our dress uniforms. The tailors had finished the alterations. I felt great pride swell up inside of me when I put on the dress uniform for the first time. I knew I was going to be a Marine, and never again would I worry about having the proper dress clothes and shoes. It was a great time of joy!

One of the last training exercises was qualifying with the rifle on the target range. I loved it. Finally, I would be able to do something I knew how to do, shoot a rifle. Remember, I said earlier that my rifle would redeem me from my swimming failure. The next three weeks were my weeks to shine. I must admit much of the training was boring to me but I had learned to listen.

The marksmanship training started with the use of a mirror sighting device. It allows you to see yourself aiming the rifle. The "snapping in" time develops proficiency in squeezing the trigger and proper breathing. It involved practicing aiming at a target and squeezing the trigger over and over again from the different firing positions — sitting, kneeling, standing and the prone position.

The next step in the training is the 900-inch range. I remember getting to feel my rifle fire a shell. All the memories of shooting on the farm ran through my mind, and I felt in my own world now. Next came the "known distance" firing at 200, 300 and 500 yards. This called for a greater effort. I learned to adjust the sights on my rifle depending on the trajectory and wind conditions, something I had not done back home by simply using what I called "Kentucky windage." This training took three weeks and the trainers were in no hurry with this time. We learned to aim at the target and shoot to kill.

Rifle range

The third week was most exciting for me, but it was not the case for some recruits who had never fired a rifle. They struggled. Many had their trigger fingers stepped on by the D.I.'s because they were not squeezing the trigger but yanking it. I guess they thought a sore finger would remind the shooter of the proper technique. The D.I.'s would have a screaming contest each time a "Maggie's drawers" would appear at the target. This meant the waving of a white flag in front of the target that means the shooter had missed the target. I had no such problems.

There was one incident that occurred on the 500 yard firing line. It was the final day and our platoon was in the final shoot off against another platoon for the high shooter trophy. I was shooting for our platoon along with Ron Medley. Ron was shooting the lights out that day and had scored a 249 out of a possible 250. The other platoon shooter had scored the same. The winning shot would come between me and the last shooter for their team. He fired first, his last shot, and hit the bull's eye. His score was 247.

I fired my last shot. The tension was thick. Usually the target would be pulled and the shot marked with a white marker indicating where the hit was located on the target. The target would come back up into sight of everyone and the score marked, five points for a bull's eye, four points for the next circle on the target, and so forth. Well, my target didn't come back up for scoring for a long time and when it did, the target workers waved the "Maggie's Drawers". My heart came up into my throat. "How could I have missed the entire target? There was no way!" The D.I. ordered me to my feet and to attention. We were shooting from the prone position. He started to chew me out but this time I was not going to take it and I screamed back at him, "No Sir!" "No Sir, what", he argued. "No Sir, it is not a miss, Sir!" I pleaded, "Sir, pull the target and check it again, Sir!"

To my great surprise he left me standing at attention and went to the field phone and asked for a re-mark of my last shot. The target went back down. He returned to me with his threats of reprisals if I was wrong. The target came back up with a bull's eye mark. I had fired my last shot through the stick that held the white marker of my previous shot. I had a 249, equaling Ron's score, but more importantly, we won the trophy.

The overall best shooter for the week won a pair of "Dress Blues". Ron and I had tied, but he won the uniform because he shot a perfect score from the 300 yard standing position and I shot one point under him. Nevertheless I was back in front of my squad and would receive my Private First Class rank when I graduated for being one of the top two shooters. The last week of the firing range also included qualifying with the .45 caliber pistols, which I did.

One last exercise remained for us, the ten mile force march to Elliott's Beach and the practical application tests. The march required each of us to carry a full combat regiment of gear — our packs, ammo, rifle and tent. It was a true test of endurance. The only problem for me was that I had come down with a cold. It later developed into pneumonia. The day we made the force march was a cold and rainy day, and I suppose the timing was right for me to come down with it. I developed a horrible cough and coughed constantly but there was no way I was going to quit. It was the only time Sergeant Leith showed any compassion. He came to me one night and asked if I wanted to go to sick bay. I knew that meant not graduating on time and I asked to be allowed to finish with our platoon. He said nothing and that was the end of it. The week was spent learning how to live in the field. It ended with squad maneuvers and enduring a four mile run in full combat gear.

Every recruit passed the week, and we marched back to the regular area, full of pride and accomplishment, and started preparing for the final regimental commander's inspection. We were just days away from becoming Marines! The regimental commander's inspection would be our final inspection. It is the end of the training test of whether each man has absorbed his training with particular emphasis placed on appearance, drill and manual of arms. Our platoon was outstanding. No demerits were issued us. We could smell the finish line. The only thing I worried about was my coughing.

Graduation day was the best of all my experiences thus far. Today I would dress in my dress uniform for the first time. I would receive my "Eagle, Globe and Anchor". This is the day I was addressed as "Marine" for the first time, and no words can explain how I felt, or how my comrades felt. We had faced the challenges and won the respect of our D.I.'s and the Marine Corps. We were now part of the great tradition of service to our beloved country and Corps.

Graduation

During this final review the outstanding men of each platoon are presented their rewards. I received my Private First Class stripe. The command, "pass in review", is given and the platoons march together for the last time. But this time we marched before the admiring eyes of many relatives and friends on hand for the ceremony. It is a magnificent sight to see. Over 750 Marines, all marching in perfect step to "Hail to the Chief" theme song being played by the Marine Corps marching band. The "colors" are presented. The regiment is brought to a halt once each platoon passes the regimental commander. Each platoon is ordered to face the front of the reviewing stand and the Senior D.I. gives the command to dismiss his platoon and it's all over. To my surprise, I never coughed once.

It was a special time of comradeship to hear Staff Sergeant Stafford dismiss us. He had gained our respect and we his respect. The next day I out posted to Camp Geiger in North Carolina. I passed back over that bridge of no return. I had become a Marine. I was physically fit except for having bronchitis, mentally strong and spiritually aware of an inner bond with a special spirit, the spirit found only in a Marine. I would never be the same as that kid who had crossed that bridge sixteen weeks earlier.

5

Advance Training At Camp Geiger

†

Camp Geiger is the next stage in the training of a Marine. The infantry training battalion's mission is to train and qualify Marines in entry level infantry military occupational specialties, in order to, provide the Operating Forces and Reserve Component with Marines capable of conducting expeditionary combat operations.

Infantry Training Battalion is a 52-day training course that develops new Marines into infantrymen who can fight, survive, and win in a combat situation. The first two weeks are a common skills package that all infantry MOS's share, where Marines receive instruction in combat marksmanship, use of grenades, military operations in jungle warfare, tactical formations, land navigation, and patrolling. Afterward, Marines receive instruction specific to their infantry MOS, regarding machine guns, mortars, reconnaissance, LAV-25s, or anti-tank warfare. The training cycle includes physical conditioning via physical training, conditioning hikes, and sustainment training in the Marine Corps martial arts program. Leadership traits and the application of the core values in every aspect of the Marine's life are also emphasized.

I arrived at Camp Geiger on June 25, 1965, late at night. I remember carrying my sea bag into the squad bay and stretching out across my bunk. I woke up in the Camp Lejeune hospital several days later with double pneumonia. My bronchitis had progressed into something much worse. I was told by the doctors that it was a miracle that I survived the last few weeks of boot camp. Still, over the next two weeks, the Navy doctors and nurses nurtured me back to health and I joined my unit in training.

Camp Geiger was a major training base closely affiliated with Camp Lejeune. Marines coming out of boot camp went there to learn to work together as a unit. The training was very thorough and intense. It was at Camp Geiger that we were introduced to live fire. It was the first exercise to conquer. It was the first time I had live rounds hitting around me. It was yet another step in molding me into the Marine tradition, men of honor, courage and commitment!

The Marine Corps was becoming my life, and I had less contact with people back home. They had their lives to live. After all, my friends were still in high school, dating, having fun, proms to attend, dances to go to, talking on the phone — all the things that normal kids did. And that is good, but it was no longer my lifestyle. I was busy too, learning about war and staying alive.

Several different training exercises took place at the live firing range. Some of these exercises were fun and some more challenging than others, but I liked most all of them. The M-60 machine gun range was exciting. Every Marine had the opportunity to fire an M-60. It fired a 7.62-mm bullet at 500-650 rounds per minute. It was deadly in a fire fight, and Mitchell and Bannister would prove that in Vietnam. I, also, learned to disassemble and reassemble it.

I was taught to fire an M-79, which was a smaller version of a hand grenade launcher. It fired a 40-mm shell and had about a five meter killing area. It reminded me of a small shot gun because it broke down at the chamber and the shell is placed into the barrel just like loading a break-down shot gun. I had a special Marine in Vietnam, Horrell, carrying this weapon and he was proficient in the use of it.

The hand grenade launcher was not as simple. It attached to the end of an M-14 rifle and was fired from the shoulder. It was much more dangerous to practice, as was throwing live M-67 hand grenades. These were thrown from a pit out into a field. The confidence building factor of throwing hand grenades involved counting to four before you threw it. It exploded at a count of five. Timing is everything in combat. Each grenade has a set fuse once the pin and spoon is released, and if you threw it too soon, the enemy would attempt to pick it up and throw it back at you. Not a good situation to find oneself in. It had a killing radius of about fifteen meters. They were one of our more useful weapons in Vietnam. This practice was nerve racking and made each of us realize it was no game we were learning. Life and death would depend on this training. I must admit the more I practiced the less concerned I was over having it explode in my hand. One Marine was lost during this training. I never heard exactly what happened except that a grenade killed him and I didn't know who he was. Using grenades became a second nature to us in Vietnam.

The next phase involved heavier weapons. Our unit learned to fire rocket launchers at dummy tanks placed at different yardages down range from our position. We learned to load the launcher and to aim and fire it. It was very rewarding to actually hit a tank. I never used one in combat, but I sure could have used one on more than one occasion.

The flame thrower was my least liked weapon to use. I suppose it reminded me too much of being burned on my leg when I was a kid. I was six years old and had found some matches lying on the counter in our kitchen. My dad was a back yard mechanic, and he had left some old motor parts soaking in a can of gasoline. It was a way of cleaning them. The problem that occurred was my striking and throwing matches ignited the can of gasoline, which caught my pants leg on fire and burned me severely. I spent many months in the hospital and needed several skin grafts to recover from it. The doctors didn't believe I would walk normally but I did. Anyway, the heat from the flame thrower reminded me of being on fire, so I spent as little time as possible practicing with it. The flame throwers were used effectively in the Pacific to route the Japanese out of their caves, but our company never used them in Vietnam. However, I wish we had them at our disposal. They would have been very useful in burning the Viet Cong out of their tunnels. I understand some Marine units used them successfully in Vietnam.

The most dangerous and difficult training was done on the mock battle field during night combat exercises. This combat obstacle course was a 100 meter long field of trenches, mud holes and barbed wire. There was an M-60 machine gunner firing live rounds at a height of twenty-five inches over the field. I remember seeing tracer rounds lighting up the night as I made my way through the course. The field was lined with explosive pits to simulate artillery shells exploding. The object of the training was to crawl through this obstacle course from one end to the other. If you rose up more than twenty-five inches the live fire would hit you. It was the closest thing to actual combat that could be created for training purposes.

I had no trouble with the training except for the barbed wire. It was very difficult to squeeze under the wire, which was only ten inches off the ground, without hooking your gear on it. The only way possible to maneuver under the wire was to use your rifle as a skid between your body and the wire. None of our Marines were hurt during this training, but some of the other units had problems. I must say it was nothing like actual combat.

It was at Camp Geiger that I had my first experience with booby traps. I was chosen to take the training, because I had completed several self-study courses in "Tactics of the Marine Corps Rifle Squad." Corporal Black was also chosen to go to the school. A corporal responded to any dangerous conditions that existed, such as disarming a booby trap while on a combat patrol. Corporals were squad leaders and had to be versed in each area of maneuvers and tactics so he was chosen to take the class. I am thankful for this training because it helped me survive disarming several of these traps while in Vietnam, though I must admit that this training was scary.

The Viet Cong manufactured these traps by using anything available to them. They especially liked to use long nails or lengths of thin steel rods, hammered flat at the ends, filed into a barbed shape, and then hammered through blocks of wood. They were then placed in camouflaged pits. Their purpose was to wound Marines who fell into the pits. The Marines attending the school learned to dismantle and disarm the traps from the least dangerous and simplest, to the most dangerous and difficult.

I started to learn the seriousness of the dangers that lie ahead, and I lost much of my innocence during these two weeks. It was a hard thing to see the carnage caused by these traps. It was the belief of the Marine Corps that all trainees see firsthand photos of the Marines who were wounded or killed by these devices. It burned a lasting impression in your mind. I always remembered seeing those photos every time I had to dismantle one of these traps in Vietnam.

Corporal Black and I became very good friends. We would continue in training until we received orders to Vietnam. He actually volunteered for Nam before I did. He was from Tennessee. Black was a devoted Marine and took everything very seriously. He had that Southern drawl that attracted everyone to him, plus he played a guitar and sang country music. He was a plenty good singer but an outstanding guitar player and could make it talk. You could not miss him since his guitar went everywhere he did. It was unusual because of its color. He had painted it black with white sides. Somehow he convinced the platoon leaders to let him carry it with him. He spent many hours entertaining us. Oftentimes I thought back to when my cousins and I would gather on Saturday evenings and make music all night. I never could play very well but my cousins were gifted musicians. I felt a bit of homesickness.

I remember during a field exercise Black received a box at mail call. The box contained a quart jar of Tennessee moonshine. He was elated and immediately took a big drink which didn't seem to bother him at all. He passed it around to several of us who were standing by and we took a drink. I mean to tell you I spit and gagged for what seemed to be for- ever. Never had I tasted such a drink. Well, everyone had a good laugh on me even though I didn't find it so funny. It burnt my throat and insides, and I felt that drink going all the way to my toes. He never let me forget that moment. Every time we passed one another he would sheepishly ask, "Want a drink?"

The booby trap school taught Black and me how to locate and disarm the main booby traps used by the Viet Cong. There were many different variations of these traps and many Marines were wounded, maimed and killed by them. The school was as close to the real thing as the Marine Corps could make it. Once we passed the classroom sessions where we learned the nomenclature and styles of booby traps, we went to the field to experience the real thing. Each of the members in the training would take their turn leading a squad on patrol. Each one of us had to walk point. That meant you were in front of the others in the squad. Each of us had a chance to dismantle any traps that we encountered. This was practiced as day and night patrols. The night patrols were especially dangerous and for the obvious reason. You can't see as well at night as you can in the daylight.

It was on one of these night patrols that I had my taste of reality while walking point. We were moving down a path that went through dense vegetation on each side when I encountered a booby trap wire across the path. That was no problem. Black was the acting squad leader and the one to dismantle it. I quietly called for him to come to the front. He located the booby trap which was a dummy hand grenade, and secured it. He moved back to his position and gave the order to move ahead. I took several steps and fell into a waist high panji trap. I probably would have died if I had been in Vietnam. These pits had sharpened bamboo stakes protruding inward from the sides of the pit. They were razor sharp and easily penetrated the skin. The pit was covered with natural elements so it was undetectable by most people.

I learned a serious lesson. Where there is one there is probably another one very close by. I was shocked, embarrassed and frightened. I aged that night and became a better fighter. Black was fit to be tied, because they

57

had to carry me back to the base camp, as if I were actually wounded. The mission wasn't accomplished and he took it personally.

This was the last exercise of this training so we were transported to our barracks by truck. I remember opening my mail of several weeks that night. I had received a letter from Barbara. She was excited about the things in her life and rightfully so. She mentioned a party that several of her girlfriends had gone to that really sounded great. Just for a brief moment I thought about being there and how different things could have been. But I realized there was no need for that kind of thinking. I had chosen my path.

However, I did have a great desire to hear her voice so I went down to the pay phones to call her. There were only a few of them near our barracks, which meant the waiting lines were always long. I waited a very long time to have my time on the phone. But her phone was busy each time I tried it. I finally gave up and went back to the barracks. It was busy most of the time, but the phone back then was a friend's life line and everyone talked for hours with each other. It was part of the culture.

Black and I rejoined our respective units at the end of this training. I rejoined my platoon just in time to practice boarding an amphibious landing craft. I found this to be profoundly different from what I had just encountered. There wasn't much to it. We climbed down a thirty foot cargo net into a boat on the ground. I would find it very different the first time I climbed down the cargo net and stepped into a real landing vessel being tossed back and forth from the ocean waves hitting the side of the ship. That would take place soon when we were assigned to the 2nd Marine Division at Camp Lejeune.

The same day, we practiced the gas chamber. This drill is part of our gas warfare training. This would not be a good experience for any of us. Each Marine had to go into a room with their gas mask on. That was phase one. Then, the instructor ordered us the remove the mask, put it back on and clear it by blowing into it. The secret is taking a big breath before removing it. Blowing into the mask clears all of the gas out of the area around your face so you can breathe normally.

The last part of the test is the dreaded part. Each Marine had to remove their mask, give name and rank, and recite their serial number, which means using up your breath, and then, re-masking. The problem is running out of air before re-masking. That means you breathe in the gas, in this case tear gas. Breathing in tear gas is an awful experience. It feels as though you will choke to death. It is nearly impossible to get the mask back onto your face and clear it of the gas. Yet, this is required to pass the test. I remember it was a scene to behold. Everyone was gagging and spitting — very humiliating. Very few were able to complete the exercise successfully, including me, but our platoon was granted permission to continue the day's training.

Finally the 52 days of training were finished at Camp Geiger, and the Marine Corps headquarters gave each of us new orders. This was the first time we were divided into different units. It was a disappointing time because we lost touch with many of our friends. Our platoon had been together since the beginning. Everyone was assigned a new duty station depending on their MOS. Some went to a mortar unit, some to tank units, a few to the Force Recon, but most of us were assigned to the 2nd Marine Division at Camp Lejeune. That is where I was assigned. My MOS was 0311, infantry, affectionately known as "jar heads."

The training at Camp Lejeune was very different from my previous training and was regimented, but that was to be expected. It involved amphibious landings and a tour of duty at Guantanamo Bay. The training at Camp Lejeune prepares Marines for combat and humanitarian missions abroad. The training base takes advantage of 156,000 acres, eleven miles of beach capable of supporting amphibious operations, thirty-two gun positions, forty-eight tactical landing zones, and eighty live fire ranges to include the Greater Sandy Run Training area.

Military forces from around the world come to Camp Lejeune on a regular basis for bilateral and NATO-sponsored exercises. There are several major Marine Corps commands and one Navy command aboard Camp Lejeune. Some tenant commands include Marine Corps Base Camp Lejeune, II Marine Expeditionary Force, 2nd Marine Division, 2nd Marine Logistics Group, and the Naval Hospital. I was assigned to the 2nd Battalion, 8th Marines, and 2nd Marine Division. I was in "F" Company, 2nd Platoon and the 1st squad.

This was a sad time having to separate from your friends in arms. I felt that I may not see many of these men again. It was nothing like what was going to happen in Vietnam. However, it was also a very exciting time. We had earned our first "leave time" and pay check which meant we could go home and visit our families and friends. I received a ten-day pass and I can tell you it did not take me long to pack and head to the Trailways bus terminal in Jacksonville, a small military town outside of the base.

I took time to go to a tailor shop in town to buy my Dress Blues. The shop was owned by a Chinese gentleman who did excellent tailor work. I went from there to the bus station, bought a ticket to Roanoke and waited for bus departure time. I went over to the juke box and ordered several songs, Ricky Nelson's "Poor Little Fool", the Beatles' "Help" and Elvis's "Crying in the Chapel". They were twenty-five cents each. Then I became acquainted with the pinball machines. I spent a lot of time playing those machines on layover during the next few days. I learned there was a way to jar them just enough to keep the pinball striking the point counters without tilting the machine. This was the key to accumulate enough points to get free games. After a while I played free until the bus boarded. There was one time at a layover in Fayetteville that I left ten free games for someone because I didn't have enough time to play them all.

"Bus 104 is now boarding for Roanoke, Virginia, at terminal six. Please have your ticket ready. Thank you." Finally, it had been six months since I left for Parris Island. I was ready to see home again.

6

My First Trip Home

I left Jacksonville, heading for home not knowing what to expect. I hadn't heard from anyone except Hazel and Barbara in weeks. It was August and in the middle of football preparation for the upcoming season. I know everyone was totally consumed by Andrew Lewis football. I was a part of that scene just last year. The bus ride home was long, and the bus stopped at every little town or at least it seemed to me that it did, but finally I started to recognize the mountains of Virginia. We passed a "Welcome to Virginia" sign. It was an inviting sight. Then we stopped in Martinsville. The next stop would be Roanoke.

I hadn't thought of where I would stay for the next few days, but I didn't feel comfortable staying at home. Hazel had shared with me that my brother had told her that dad had a woman staying with them — it was Arlene. He would later marry her. So I caught the city transient bus and rode to my friend Steve Brown's house. They lived near my old house in West Salem. I remember knocking on the door and wondering if I would be received with open arms. I should have known that I would receive a grand welcome from them. Dr. Brown, Steve's mom, answered the door and welcomed me with a big hug. "We have missed you!" she said. "Hey everyone guess who is here? It's Philip, home from the service." That sounded so strange to me, "home from the service." It was late by the time we finished talking and them updating me on everything and everyone. I wanted to go see Barbara and Hazel but decided to wait until tomorrow.

I didn't sleep well that night in anticipation of seeing Barbara and Hazel. Nonetheless, morning came as always, and I had breakfast and headed for Salem. The walk seemed longer than I remembered it and I felt out of place — a Marine walking along the sidewalk dressed in a Marine uniform. It seemed I should have a car for transportation or something. I had called Hazel so she was expecting me. It was Saturday morning and very early, around eight o'clock so no one was awake except her and Durwood. She had her instant coffee ready and we sat and talked for a long time. I kept straining my ears listening for Barbara to come down from upstairs. Finally she popped in and gave me a big hug. It felt so good. She was as beautiful as ever. She commented on how much I had changed and how nice I looked in uniform. She couldn't stay long because her friend, Mary Ann, was dropping by and they were going to the library. I asked if I could see her later and she said to call her.

The morning was just about gone and I needed to see Mike. Durwood was nice enough to drive me to my house to see him. I dreaded spending time with Arlene but figured I would make the best of it for Mike's sake. Durwood cautioned me to keep my nose clean and he advised me to not do anything stupid. I guess he could see I was still very angry at that entire mess. He was a good man and great father, and his care for me meant a lot. We pulled up to the house and I got out. He pulled off and blew the horn at me.

Mike wasn't expecting me. He was surprised to see me at the door. I actually hugged him and we went to his room to talk. Many things had happened since I left for the Marines. He was unhappy, and in serious trouble with school and a few older boys who were bullying him. He felt trapped, and I could sense his anger and hurt. He wanted me to help him with the boys who were troubling him so we started to leave the house to go and find them. Dad saw me and made some kind of comment. I ignored him and her as Mike and I left. It seemed these boys liked to hang out at a place called Lawrence's Store. It was only a short walk from where we lived on Wildwood Road.

Sure enough, they were there when we walked up. My temper immediately took control of me and I threatened to kill them where they were standing if they opened their mouth even once. The word "kill" had become part of my vocabulary. They believed me and said nothing. I told them that Mike was my brother and if I had to come back looking for them, I would hurt them seriously. Then, I closed the space between us by stepping toward them. My training had taught me to move within striking range of your enemy and I saw them as the enemy. I was close enough to them to hit them. I said to each of them pointedly, "Do you understand exactly what I am telling you?" They nodded that they understood. Mike and I went inside and bought a coke and left. He had many issues after I left to return to Camp Lejeune but not with them.

I didn't know how to relate to Mike except in situations like the one I described. I was still a very distant and angry person, but we did talk about the neighborhood and dad's drinking. Things were no better, and he said dad brought Arlene to the house to clean and take care of things around the house. He also said dad had nightmares about mom's death and couldn't stay alone in the house. I told Mike that was good and he was getting what he deserved. I asked Mike if he would like to go shooting rifles before I left but he told me dad had sold all my guns, one more reason to have nothing to do with him.

My next stop was Andrew Lewis High School. A very interesting visit took place at the high school. I went there to visit with Coach Joyce. He was surprised to see me and very taken back with what the Marines had done for me. He noticed my weight gain and muscular strength and commented on it, in fact. We talked about the Marines and the football team. He introduced me to the guys as if I didn't already know them. It was a good visit.

Then, he told me to follow him to the principal's office. I felt awkward about it. Our visit was a great surprise to Mr. Barnett. I could see he was pleased to see me, and he definitely noticed my uniform and highly shined shoes. I think he was pleased to see my maturity. It was a good visit. He wished me a good visit while I was in Salem. The three of us never met again, but I am thankful for the influence both of these men had on my life.

I felt I needed to visit with my favorite aunt, Aunt Virginia, and Walt, her husband, who had been career Air Force. They lived in Roanoke, and have two daughters, Brenda and Karen. They insisted I stay a few days with them which I gladly did. Both girls went to Jefferson High School, a big rivalry to Andrew Lewis, so we had fun poking japs at one another. They hated to see me go when I headed back to North Carolina.

Barbara and I did go out on a date. We went to a movie but I don't remember what we saw. I was too much in awe of her. We doubled dated with Steve and Mary Ann. We had a good time together and I enjoyed it, and I think she did too. The time flew by and before I knew it I was on the bus headed back to another adventure and more serious training. I would come back to Salem several times on weekend passes while I was at Camp Lejeune, and Barbara and I would date each time. The ride back to Jacksonville seemed short, maybe because I slept most of the way. I reported to my new unit and my training started immediately. It would last fourteen months until I volunteered for Vietnam.

7

Training At Camp Lejeune – Becoming Mentally Ready For Combat

August was hot in North Carolina. The next phase of my training was field maneuvers — war games. That meant we had to force-march everywhere we went in the bush. Sometimes these marches would be ten miles in length. The trainers attempted to make it as close to the real thing as possible. The only difference was we used blanks instead of live ammo. It was sort of like the war games I played as a kid back home, and I liked the adventure. I look back on things now and I realize how foolish those thoughts were, but I think it was being caught in a teenager's body with a man's mission to accomplish. But there is one thing I know for a fact. My fellow Marines and I were being molded into fighting men. Every instinct and initiative was concentrated on killing the enemy and surviving. Every day that passed we learned to trust the one on the right and left of us. We started to sense that we would never be left behind in combat. If necessary, we would die for each other!

This was the time in our training that I could see all the smaller training times coming together. For example, our regiment put out to sea to practice amphibious landing assaults. The practice on dry land of climbing up and down the cargo nets paid off. It was the most exciting thing that I had done to date. Climbing over the rail on the troop transport ship and ascending down the cargo net into the LCP-R landing boat was hair-raising. The ship was moving with the ocean waves and the landing boat was pitching up and down some six feet. It would collide with the side of the ship and bounce off, leaving a gap between it and the ship. If a Marine fell between the boat and the ship, they would surely drown. The trick was to time your release of the net when the boat reached its apex and was against the ship. I only got one chance at it because there were Marines climbing down the cargo net right behind me. When all the Marines were in their boat, it pulled off and joined the other boats that would make up the different assault waves.

The Landing Craft (LCP-R) was constructed from plywood and was a shallow-draft, barge-like boat that ferried a platoon-sized complement of thirty-six men to shore at nine knots. It had two machine gun positions in front and a drop down ramp. That was not the best scenario because the drop-down ramp was the only way of leaving the boat to assault the beach, and the enemy would aim at the ramp because we had no protection.

I will never forget my first experience hitting the beach, as it is called in the Corps. The coxswain dropped the ramp on a sand dune about fifty meters from the beach. I was the fourth man off the ramp. Everything seemed good for the first few meters. We were in ankle deep water. The beach head was about fifty meters in front of us. Then, the sand bar ended and the bottom dropped out, and I was in water up to my nose. I had flashbacks to Parris Island and the incident in the pool. Fear gripped my heart but I was able to bounce up and down, half swimming, as I moved toward the beach and soon I was safe on shore, exhausted but safe. I was not alone. Every one of us was dragging but we managed to make our way to the sand dunes and set up cover fire for the other Marines coming ashore. It was great training but it was not used in Vietnam. Instead, we helicoptered into position, but the experience that day proved to me that I had matured as a person. I didn't panic as I had done in boot camp, and it was a huge confidence builder. Each new experience strengthened my resolve to be a good Marine.

The days were long and hard at Camp Lejeune, and we rose early in the morning and trained until late into the evening. The one difference from this routine as compared to our previous training was that at the end of the day we could do as we wanted. There were many things to do. Some guys went to town, some played basketball or football, some rested and some studied for the promotion tests. I chose to play basketball and study and my hard work and study paid off. My superiors seemed to put their trust in my leadership, plus they liked the fact that I was demanding and strict on myself. Failure was not an option for me.

The Marine Corps had become my place to express my anger and patriotism. I always had a deep sense of patriotism, even in grade school. I identified with the patriots of Virginia, such Robert E. Lee and Stonewall Jackson. I thought of it as childish thinking as I grew older but now I was revisiting those thoughts and understanding myself in a different light. Sometimes I couldn't even understand which attribute controlled me, my anger or patriotism, but I liked it!

Our battalion shipped out of Camp Lejeune in late October, heading for maneuvers on an island known as Vieques. I will never forget that deployment. First, we missed the cold weather and training in the freezing temperatures of North Carolina. Marines who had been stationed there had told us about the horror of that possibility. However, more important than that, I participated in war games that were as close, as possible, to the fighting that the Marines endured in the South Pacific in WWII. The experience let me see the power of the Marine Corps fighting units. I didn't realize it then but in Vietnam this power sustained me in battle, and was a mental preparation for combat. It was a snapshot of developing my mental toughness.

This was the first time I had been out of sight of land. We shipped out in the early afternoon on a beautiful day and the ocean was calm and deep blue in color. Most of the Marines on the ship were hanging on the guard rails watching the land disappear, the waves and the ocean buoys passing by us. The sailors suggested we go down to the quarter-deck where the view was much better, and many of us made the mistake of doing that. The ocean was right there at you and you could almost reach out and touch it.

That is all I remember for several days. I became deathly sick with my head swirling in every direction. I lost everything in me, but I was not by myself. Most of us were too sick to make muster call. My sickness passed in time and I was able to experience the most awesome display of military power I had seen to date. The experience of the next few days would overwhelm all of us. I would finally understand the purpose of all the physical, mental and combat preparation of the last months of training. I started to think nothing or no one could stand against us in combat.

Vieques was not only a place for Marines to practice amphibious landings; it was also a live firing range for the Navy gunners. While I was sick, with most of my fellow Marines, we had joined a naval fleet of battle ships and destroyers. Our troop carrier was part of a major display of combat readiness for the news reporters, who were there in great numbers. One of them was assigned to my platoon, and he told us that President Johnson wanted Americans to see firsthand that we were ready to fight and were as strong as the Marines of past generations. I can speak for every Marine there when I say our pride swelled within us!

The day of the assault on the beaches started at breakfast, and there was an eerie strangeness about it all. We had the traditional breakfast of meat and eggs that was fed to the Marines before they assaulted the islands in the Pacific. I was a squad leader, and the other squad leaders and I met with our platoon leader and received instruction about our objective, which was the first time I had met in a formal setting with ranking officers. There would be many in Vietnam. We would be the third wave going in and would reinforce the second wave with an objective of securing the western end of the island.

I returned to my squad and briefed them on what would happen. The ammunition was passed out and each of us prepared ourselves to move up to the boarding area. The ammunition was blank ammo. Suddenly our ship shook from the percussion of the big guns firing from the ships near to us. The loudness of the big guns firing was deafening to those of us who had never been around this much fire power before. Soon we were climbing the steps to the loading deck, while the guns from the battleship and destroyer nearest to us kept firing. We could see the explosions on shore, and my first thought was one of panic. "Surely they will cease firing before we hit the beach!" I had been taught to trust my fellow comrade in combat, but was now the time to apply that training?

Everything went like clockwork with each platoon of our company, "F" Company, being commanded to move into position and to climb over the side and descend down the cargo nets to the LCP-R's below. The ocean was rough, and it was not easy getting into the landing crafts. Several of our Marines were hurt when their feet were caught between the ship and the nets. They still rode the boats to shore but didn't depart from them with the rest of us. When the last Marine in our unit, who happened to be Smitty, was in the LCP-R landing boat I heard the engine accelerate and we moved away from the ship and headed to the other landing crafts in our landing wave.

It seemed we would circle forever. Each wave of boats circled in tight formations until time to go ashore, and then the coxswain turned the boat and sped toward land. It was different than our earlier training assaults off the coast of North Carolina. This time he was really moving with the boat seemingly jumping from wave top to wave top. Everyone was holding on and I could see anticipation of not knowing what was going to happen in everyone's eyes. The guns of the big ships were still firing! The machine gunners on our boat started firing and I heard the coxswain tell our platoon leader, Second Lieutenant Henry, to prepare to disembark. He gave the order to "Lock and Load!" The ramp fell and we rushed the beach in shallow water. My heart was beating a hundred times a minute, and I thanked God by this time the shell explosions were deep within the island and not near the beach.

The first and second waves had moved inland 400 or 500 meters toward their objective and were turning westward. We turned westward and forced marched several miles to a position on the left of the 1st Platoon. It was a demanding march in the sand, carrying eighty-five pounds of combat-ready gear, but we had to arrive at our objective before the other platoons. We would act as a blocking force to engage retreating enemy units, which the 1st and 3rd Platoons would force out of their positions. We dug in and set up fields of fire for each squad and began the waiting process. Part of a tank corps joined us later that day. Our company had handled itself with proficiency and we spent the night in that position. The next morning we moved eastward and met up with the 1st and 3rd Platoons. The march back to the beach was easy. We boarded the LCP-R's and returned to the troop transport ship and the exercise was complete. All of us had a sense of great accomplishment. We believed in ourselves and were actually part of a combat ready regiment. It was a defining moment, and we felt great!

My next training took place at Guantanamo Bay which was located on the southern end of Cuba and very close to Vieques. It was supposed to be a time of rest but ended up being five months of more duty. I could hardly believe we were protecting an area where President Kennedy had showed such courage in backing down the Soviets. The Marines stood guard duty over the naval base there in the region. It was hot and boring and none of us liked our stay there.

The most interesting thing was the sand crabs. They were enormous in size compared to normal sand crabs I had seen, about the size of a baseball. When they walked they made this clicking sound, like you would imagine a walking skeleton sounding like. That sound traveled for hundreds of meters at night. Sometimes it was difficult to distinguish them from approaching people. They kept us on our toes for sure.

The important thing about this duty was we had live ammo in our rifles. The Cubans were just across the wire from us and posed a possible threat to the base security. This was the first time we actually had the potential to shoot someone if necessary. I realize now that it was a large step in maturing as a responsible Marine. My thoughts were so much different, knowing I had live ammunition in my rifle and it raised my accountability to a higher level. It seemed everything that happened brought me closer to actual combat. Our training and required duty was more and more professional. I was more comfortable with who I was becoming. I was responsible and knew my actions carried serious consequences.

The guard duty was important but it was very mundane. However, there were some enlightening experiences. The beaches at Gitmo were outstanding. The sand was white, and the water was a magnificent blue. I spent most of my spare time on the beach or in the water. Also, several comical things happened, such as my horseback riding experience. It ended with me in a cactus tree with serious thorns puncturing my body. It seemed the horse had a mind of its own and when I said "stop" the horse interpreted that as go. When he finally stopped, I was tossed over his neck into the cactus. I walked gingerly for some time.

Finally the time passed and we headed for home. We arrived back at Camp Lejeune in late March 1966. It was amazing for me to conceive of the idea that I had been a Marine for nearly one year, but even more surprising, I was promoted to the rank of Lance Corporal on April 1. None of my friends back home could even envision the vast change in me or all I had experienced in this year. I felt as if I had lost the innocence of a small town country boy, even though I was only seventeen years old. I had a new life, a career and honor, and I was proud to be a United States Marine and an American!

It was good to be back at Camp Lejeune. Our unit was given leave time, and I had fifteen days left that I could use to go home, but I decided to go to South Carolina with a friend, Private Rene Lamourant. He wanted me to meet his family and I really didn't feel like going to my home. Things there were tense, and I could tell by Hazel's letters that she was worried about my safety and the possibility of my going to Vietnam. I had made the mistake of mentioning that I wanted to volunteer for Vietnam, so I avoided the uneasiness of the whole thought by not going home.

8

My Second Trip Home-Spiritual Awareness Found In Waycross

*T*he trip to Waycross, South Carolina, was very enlightening for me. I had a transformation of thinking you might say. I learned about the third element of becoming a Marine. The recruiter said I would become physically fit, mentally sound and spiritually grounded, and he was right! Every Marine goes through the process.

My friend was my radio man in my squad and a very likeable person; and he especially was proud of being a Marine, more so than most. I understood his need to be accepted by his comrades when I saw his home, and I was shocked, to be honest. His house was no more than a shack, and I was not sure why it remained standing. The porch was sagging, and the screens on the windows were torn. Knowing him, it was not what I expected but I realized why he chose the Marines. It offered him a way to overcome his circumstances and develop mental toughness. Don't misunderstand me. He was happy and proud to present me to his widowed mother and siblings, and it was then that I realized a home is not a wooden structure. It is the people who live in it that count. It's much like the Marine Corps. It's not the name Marine that makes it great, but the men who serve under the name.

This was the third home I had ever visited that prayed at meal times — the Browns, Hazel and now here. This time the prayers meant more to me, maybe because I heard a mother praying for her son's safety and her gratefulness for the bounty her family enjoyed. I didn't see much bounty, but they did. It seemed as though her prayers reached right into Heaven.

It was later that night I heard her praying in her room. I was on the front porch with Lamourant's little sister and brother. They thought I was the greatest thing since ice cream and insisted on me telling them all about the Marine Corps. Her window was ajar, and I couldn't help ignoring the kids and listening to her prayer. I am not sure but I think she was crying as she prayed. I actually believed she believed in what she was asking God to do for her son and me by pleading with Him to keep us safe.

This was the spiritual piece I personally needed to remold me from a civilian to a Marine. Not every Marine needed this element in their life to be strong, but I needed it, and this would complete the new me. Maybe I needed a higher connection because of my unforgiving nature and angry attitude. I have thought this many times. Anyway, this experience would carry me through combat.

The Marine recruiter had mentioned it to my father and the D.I.'s had mentioned spiritual discipline. The chaplains were always talking about it. Hey, I thought I had a handle on such things, but my problem was misunderstanding the idea of spirituality. I understood everyone as meaning "esprit de corps". I guess part of it was that spirit, the inner-spirit to fight for a cause, but this meant something different, more religious in nature.

It was somewhat comforting to me. Johnson and I would talk about it at a church one evening while in Vietnam. I didn't believe in Christ but I did respect God. It was only a connection with God that I felt I needed.

I can't explain it but I felt different after my time with Lamourant's family. Don't get me wrong, I had never denied God, per se. I just didn't place much thought into religion. I wasn't disrespectful or any such thing. I just didn't understand, because religion had been a thing of convenience for me. It helped me to feel good, but there was no strength in it for me. However, now I lay awake thinking about God and if He really could protect people, like Mrs. Lamourant believed. This sense of protection from a Higher Being is a much needed element in combat.

I started to remember some of the things Durwood and Hazel shared with me about inner-peace and fortitude that God could give to those in need. I fell asleep later that night thinking about the prayer of Hazel for me. It seemed very close to the prayer of Lamourant's mom. My pride kept me from speaking to Mrs. Lamourant about my feelings, because I was afraid Rene might think less of me as a Marine, so I told Lamourant I needed to go home after staying with them for only a few days. He borrowed his mom's car and took me to the bus station and I was on the way home in a few hours.

It was a long ride to Salem from Waycross, South Carolina. In fact, it took a full day and most of the night. It was a long time for me to have to think about what had just happened, but I was confused and really needed some answers. I had a sick feeling in my stomach about going to Vietnam with this uneasiness in my thoughts about God, and I knew if anyone could help me it would be Hazel. The bus stopped at a small town somewhere in North Carolina, and remained there long enough for me to call Hazel and let her know I was on my way home for a few days. The joy and excitement in her voice was a great uplift to my spirit. The bus arrived in Roanoke very early, around 3:30 in the morning, so I decided to sleep on the bench in the terminal until daybreak.

It is amazing how nothing had changed since the last time I was home — the transit bus route, the scenery, everything. I spent several days talking to Hazel even though I stayed with the Browns at night. Mike and I spent some time together, but not much. I was able to see Barbara and we talked, but my focus was easing this nagging frustration about God and prayer. Hazel was very patient with me and willing to discuss my many issues.

It didn't take her very long to direct our discussions to my relationship with Christ. I felt very uneasy about her references to Him as the answer to my questions but I listened. She wanted me to be sure I knew Him, as she referred to it. I suppose I was less than honest with her when I answered her concerns with what I felt she wanted to hear; still I was confused why God would allow such tragedies in life to occur, such as my mom's death, and why He would be interested in a Marine. Hazel was a very wise woman of God, and she let me do the talking and the questioning. I suppose she knew I just needed to vent my frustrations and anger. It was strange but in her silence I found direction and was able to settle my dilemma in my own way. "Would God answer prayers for everyone, especially moms?" I figured time would tell.

I came to realize that Hazel was my mom now and I needed to know she would be praying for me so I asked her straight out, "If I go to Vietnam, will you pray for my safety?" I have never forgotten her response. She said, "Every waking moment! Prayer is what moves the hand of God on our behalf." I believe the prayers of mothers saved us from total annihilation in Vietnam.

Then one of those defining moments in life took place as she prayed for me that very moment. Her prayer almost expressed the same concerns of Mrs. Lamourant. She prayed, "Keep Philip safe and all his buddies!" She thanked God for allowing me to be in her life. I am so thankful she had her eyes closed because at that moment I had tears in mine. I choked back my emotions before she finished her prayer. Nothing about Jesus was settled but I was convinced her prayers would keep God watching over me. That limited faith would carry me through the horror of combat. I think each Marine comes to this point in different ways. We spent the remainder of the day enjoying each other's company, and I had the peace I needed.

The ride back to Camp Lejeune gave me time to process the last days. Many questions still filled my mind. I wondered if my mom prayed and if she did, for what kind of things. I wished I could have heard her pray. I knew my father didn't pray. He didn't have it in him. I tried to envision what my mom would think of me in uniform. I thought about my friendship with Barbara and wondered if it would ever be more than just a friendship. Mike was always on my mind, and I worried about his future. I reviewed all my training and questioned if I was ready to volunteer for Vietnam. It seemed like the right thing to do. "Why become a Marine if you were not going to fight?" I think I settled that question on that return trip back to the base. I decided to volunteer as soon as I finished the last leg of our training cycle, helicopter assault tactics.

9

Chopper Assault Training

Helicopter assault training was my favorite time spent in training. I loved to fly and I remember the first time I flew in a chopper. I felt the adrenalin flow through my veins. I remember the fear of the blades spinning just a few feet above my head as I approached the chopper to board it. The thrill of lifting off the ground and then turning sharply to the side was exhilarating. I looked out the door of the chopper and watched the trees going by below us, as I felt the wind coming in through the door and hitting me in the face. I will never forget that moment. Just for a moment I wished I was a chopper pilot. It was so much like being home with no cares in the world and flying in Hilton's bi-wing airplane, but those were the good memories of flying. The training itself was intense and dangerous, and we had a Marine break his leg and several sprained their ankles during the training. The training included both classroom and field work.

The first thing I realized when dealing with helicopter assaults is that I probably would land in a "hot zone", which means there are enemy fighters already in position and the chopper is their target. Each chopper could carry about twenty Marines handily and up to thirty if necessary and that was usually the case in Vietnam. A chopper is a very easy target for ground fire and rockets to hit, which made it vitally important that each Marine knows exactly what he is to do once the chopper arrives in the LZ (landing zone). Each squad has a specific mission to accomplish at the LZ.

The squad is to disembark as quickly as possible and move immediately to its position on the parameter of the LZ and set up its field of fire. Each Marine has a certain portion of the terrain in front of him that he must cover with fire if his squad is receiving incoming fire. His fire patterns will overlap the Marine's pattern of fire to his right and left so that no area is missed. The same practice is true for each member of the squad. The crisscrossing of fire power is deadly to any attacking enemy soldier. Marines are famous for their accuracy in this maneuver.

The LZ is abandoned once the entire platoon is on sight. It is the mission of the Marine Company to advance against the enemy, not stay in one place especially in a place that can be honed in upon by enemy mortars or artillery. The practice of marking the LZ with red smoke made it easy for the enemy to concentrate their fire on the incoming choppers, so speed is of the essence.

The crew chief on each chopper was a vital person in the equation, since he would tell the squad leader where the enemy is located and the intensity of their fire power. He also made sure everyone left the chopper in a hurry. He would let us know the time factor involved in arriving on sight. That helped us say our last prayers, lock and load our rifle, and prepare to move.

The classroom training was very important, and the Marine instructors, as usual, were very honest and forthcoming in their remarks. They made sure we understood what was ahead of us. They explained that as infantrymen charge out of helicopters during daytime landings, confusion reigns for a couple minutes as leaders attempt to orient themselves and link up with Marines from other helicopters. Every landing is difficult because some helicopters may have turned back for mechanical reasons, some may be shot down, and few land exactly where they should. Then, they explained that the wind, dust, and noise helicopters generate causes further confusion, not to mention enemy fire. However, according to them, the biggest danger is mid-air collisions as helicopters land and take-off in confined areas. I think everything they said was true but I, personally, never saw a mid-air collision in Vietnam. If just one helicopter goes down in an LZ panic may ensue, so every Marine must be prepared to do what it takes to accomplish the mission.

We also learned the troop-carrying choppers always came in low, tree top high into the LZ. This was to surprise the enemy, but it was another way that the chopper pilots could stay out of sight for as long as possible. The trees and jungle acted like a barrier for them. It very seldom worked as planned and the enemy was usually waiting with heavy machine gun and small arms fire, which was even more the reason for us to get to our positions as soon as possible. The emphasis was placed on getting out of the chopper, away from it, keeping low and moving. It was the Viet Cong and NVA's job to pin us down, and our job was to not let that happen.

Once the classroom instruction concluded, we were introduced to the choppers. The instructors, usually pilots, took us around the aircraft and explained its weaknesses and strengths. We were allowed to sit in the choppers and ask questions. Many of the instructors were Vietnam veterans and were able to answer our questions from their experience of being in combat.

It seemed childish at first when I started my hands-on training. Our company went to the field and practiced loading and unloading from a chopper that remained stationary on the ground. I practiced leaving the chopper and taking up my position on the parameter of the LZ just like I was taught to do in the classroom. I didn't really appreciate all those mock runs until I first experienced the real thing in a combat situation. This part of my training lasted several days.

Finally, it came time to actually practice what we had learned. A similar scenario existed as that of our amphibious landing training. Our battalion would assault a position held by another Marine unit acting as the enemy. This would be a two week long deployment. We went into the exercise with full combat gear, and our mission was to find and eliminate the enemy. We were given a specific target to capture and the coordinates of that target. The unique thing about this exercise was that it brought into play our entire training to this point — day tactics, night maneuvers, compass use, camouflage techniques, calling in artillery and air strikes, re-supplying our units and helicopter tactics. We were preparing for Vietnam. The only thing lacking in this exercise was an amphibious assault.

Nothing out of the ordinary took place, and all of our units accomplished their goals. I must say the first time I landed in the LZ with more than one chopper landing together was an experience. It was just as I had been instructed. Everyone was screaming orders and Marines were responding partly out of an awareness of their training and partly out of panic. It was nothing like the mock runs I made earlier. Vietnam would be even more confusing and frustrating. My squad did its thing and we met up with the other squads and continued through the exercise.

The extraction from the area was another experience. I thought it would be easy to run out to a chopper resting on the ground, climb in and be on my way, but it wasn't that simple. The ending scenario of the exercise included our unit being the last one to leave the mock combat area, and that meant we had to secure the LZ and maintain superiority over the advancing enemy force.

I knew the proper procedure to accomplish that part of the equation but I never had to run to a chopper dressed in full combat gear and board a chopper that was only going to stay in place for a short minute or two. I was the last one to climb into the chopper that picked up my squad. The squad leader was always the last one to board. The problem was the chopper lifted off before I was fully inside of it. I had one knee on the floor of the chopper but the rest of me was outside of it. I lost my hold and was about to fall when my buddies grabbed me and yanked me into the chopper. Once again, I experienced the soundness of our training. Marines stay in a state of readiness and they are always faithful. I rolled over on the floor of the chopper, let my feet hang out of the door opening and shouted "Semper Fi". My squad thundered back, "Hoo-ra!" The Crew Chief wasn't very happy but the rest of us were elated.

It was May, and the next few months would be long and depressing. We had finished our training and there was nothing left to do but repeat it all over again or volunteer for some other duty station or MOS. Most of us wanted to go Vietnam but Division was not asking or assigning anyone to go. The thought of staying at Camp Lejeune didn't appeal to me, and to make things worse, my company was assigned guard duty for the regiment. That meant standing guard day and night for the next three months. No Marine likes guard duty. It's nearly as bad as mess duty.

The summer dragged by until finally, August arrived and our battalion received orders to re-qualify with small arms. Normally requalification with small arms wouldn't take a full month but since our entire battalion was scheduled we took the whole month of August. I re-qualified as an expert riflemen and pistol shooter.

It was at the end of August 1966 that I was told I was going to Vietnam. August was a good month for me. I was promoted to the rank of corporal and was going to fight for my country, but I didn't receive direct orders to leave for Vietnam until November.

September was a typical month for a Marine battalion stationed at Camp Lejeune and especially between training cycles. The emphasis was placed on marching, physical fitness and inspections. Our battalion took the PRT exam. There was not much to it. Each Marine had to run a three-mile course in twenty-eight minutes or less, do twenty pull-ups and fifty abdominal crunches. We underwent our company barracks inspection and regiment rifle and gear inspections. There was free time for us to enjoy the fruits of our labor making it an easy month.

I was relieved of my duty with my battalion, along with fifty or more other Marines, and had nothing to do except kill time during October. Each day I checked with headquarters to see if my orders had been cut and each day they would tell me to be patient. Occasionally others would hear good news and be gone. Corporal Black was one. The time seemed to crawl by.

Finally on Thursday, November 10, on the Marine Corps birthday, at 0800 hours I received my orders. I was given until December 5 to report to

Travis Air Force Base in California, so I packed my gear and headed home to Virginia to spend some time with my family and friends.

This time instead of taking the Trailway bus, I went to the outdoor flick (movie) parking lot. It was around eight in the morning and I found someone heading in my direction. Oftentimes it was easy to find a ride with a Marine who had a car on base who was going on leave. This Marine was going to Bristol, Tennessee, which meant he would go through Roanoke on the way. It was perfect. I paid him twenty bucks for the ride, and several of us were packed into his old Chevrolet. The trip took seven hours, but was much faster than the bus ride. I felt lucky because he dropped me off at the beginning of Wildwood Road in West Salem. I lived on that road, plus it was in the afternoon, so no one was home. Mike was out and Dad was working.

10

The Time Was Drawing Near

The door to the house was unlocked so I went in and waited for someone to arrive. Mike arrived home before dad so we had some private time to talk. I told him I was headed for Vietnam, but to my surprise it didn't seem to bother him. I had expected him to be sad or something, but he showed no emotion. Time and his circumstances had hardened him. I realized it and was both glad and worried. I didn't want him to be like me, so hard that no emotions were ever shown, and yet I knew he would have to be strong in order to survive his home conditions. I asked him if things had changed with dad and he said they were worse. He conveniently didn't tell me that he was in serious trouble with the law and the school system. His life was about to change as dramatically as mine but in a much different direction. He would spent time in several correctional institutions for teens. Later, he would join the Marine Corps.

Dad and Arlene came home after his work, and you can imagine their surprise to see me sitting in their kitchen. I remember his look. He seemed to be small in my eyes. I towered over him. He asked how I was doing and I kept it nice by replying I was good and that I had orders to Vietnam and would be leaving town on the December 4. I don't remember much of the conversation and nothing important was said. He did wish me luck. I didn't stay for supper and that was probably a good thing. I couldn't imagine sitting at mom's table and another woman serving the meal.

The visit ended abruptly when he referred to Arlene as our mother. That did not sit well with me, and I asked him to step into the next room where I told him, "It would be a cold day in hell before she would be our mother. And the next time I heard her called that it would be the last time she or he would draw a breath!" He didn't have anything to say and it was a good thing because I may have hurt him seriously if he had spoken. The hatred between us was thick enough to cut it with a knife. I told Mike I would see him later and left. That was the last time I would see him until I came home on leave after Vietnam.

I walked out to the main road and caught a ride into Salem with a stranger. I think he regretted picking me up. My attitude wasn't the best, and my heart was still pounding, and I know he thought I was drinking. I could hardly speak. I settled down before he let me off on Main Street. He wished me luck and I thanked him for the ride. I had a few blocks to walk before I came to Barbara's house, and that helped me regain my composure. I had a date with Barbara and I didn't want to mess that up.

Hazel and the entire crew were pleased to see me. In fact, they acted like I had been missing for years. I must admit it felt good. I remember distinctly that Barbara answered the door. She hardly ever did that. She hugged me for what seemed like an eternity. Don't get me wrong, I loved every second of it. Durwood shook my hand along with Derby, Barbara's younger brother. Regina, Barbara's little sister, was a little shy but she, too, gave me a hug. Hazel was last to hug me but it was special. Words cannot express the understanding between us at that moment. Love, trust, care, encouragement, concern and fear all were part of that moment.

Barbara and I didn't spent much time there. Steve and his date arrived and we joined them to go a movie. Barbara was different somehow. I can't explain it but she was perfect for the time. She was genuine with me and honest; maybe because she knew where I was going, but I like to think she really loved me. But we were young and she had her life to live. The date went quickly and before we knew it we were back at her house. I stayed the night and slept on the couch. We spent a lot of time together during those days and were very close.

The next day I went to my Aunt Virginia's house to spend some time with them. They, too, were excited to see me. Walt and Virginia had an understandable concern on their face about the entire Vietnam thing, but the girls, Brenda and Karen, were their usual fun-loving selves. I stayed with them for several days. I don't recall any earth shattering talks, just being able to enjoy their fellowship.

Aunt Virginia suggested I should visit the family in Floyd or the country as we referred to it. The rest of my cousins, aunts and uncles lived in Floyd. Steve and I drove there and spent an entire day visiting with them and shooting rifles. Shooting back then was almost a national holiday. I remember David, my older cousin, giving me a hand full of dollar bills. In fact, he gave me every dollar he had in his wallet, and insisted that I take it and have fun. He had spent a tour in the Army and knew how tight money was for a soldier. I didn't think much of it at that moment but later realized everyone was trying to offer me something that might give them a sense of being part of me; they were afraid I might not come back home alive. It was a sobering thought for me!

The days flew by, and it became time to leave. There was one more thing I needed to do. There was a very large rock formation on Fort Lewis Mountain. This rock is visible from miles around. That was the mountain range behind my house in West Salem. I wanted to climb the mountain and go to it one more time. It was a place all of us neighborhood boys would go during the summer. We were kids but it offered us an adventurous challenge. Supposedly the outlaw Dalton gang hid a treasure near it and it became our home away from home. The rock had a cave near it where we would camp and a running stream where we would swim and have fun. I remembered it was very difficult climbing. The brush was very thick and there were no trails. I used my compass that the Marines had issued me and plotted a course and made the climb. No one went with me. I wanted to experience it alone.

I made the climb in very good time and reached it by noonday. The adventure was as I remembered it as a kid. The rock was massive and overlooked my house, Salem, and as far you could see — most of Roanoke. I was proud of myself for being able to use my compass to find it. It is hidden from sight because of the terrain until you are upon it. I didn't realize, at the time, how valuable that compass would turn out to be in Vietnam.

It was a cold November day, and a strong wind was blowing across the face of the rock. The cold was eased somewhat by the sun rays shining down on my body. I sat down in the middle of it and almost fell asleep. I sat there for more than an hour and I rehearsed in my mind all that had happened in my life. I thought about all the childhood pranks, times the guys and I got into trouble for stealing wood and nails from the highway department to use to build a tree house, and the time we had to return a Miller Tire Company tire we stole to use to float the Roanoke River. I thought of carving Barbara's name in the big Sycamore tree out back of our house and the hours I spent panting over Hayley Mills. Thoughts of mom crying at night and her hard work cleaning the house and our clothes haunted my thoughts. I reminisced about playing football for Andrew Lewis and the fun times I had there. I even remembered Miss Maxwell and her determination to teach me algebra, and I chuckled when I remembered carrying Barbara in my arms down a road after a day of hiking. She claimed she couldn't walk any farther and I believed her. I wondered what would happen to Mike and our dog Smokey. Man, those were good days and I realized they were in the past, and I couldn't reclaim them. I suppose a hundred memories flooded my mind sitting there looking down on the valley until a hawk screeching, as he flew by, interrupted my thinking and I lost my train of thought. It was for the best.

God occupied much of my thinking. I wouldn't say I prayed but I did think about God. This time there were no questions for Him, just a seeking of His peace. I knew I was an angry person and that I lived my life with a chip on my shoulder, daring anyone to knock it off, and for the first time I acknowledged it to myself. I realized it was time to be honest with myself. I guess I figured God would make me do that anyway.

I made God and myself a promise that day at that special place on the mountain. I would represent the Corps with pride, honor and courage, and if necessary I would die for my country. You might say I had an early "fox-hole" experience or a "mountain top" experience as religious people would say. I wanted the favor of God and I felt the warm fuzzies envelop my body. That sounds silly, but I thought about it many times during combat. I believe it was on that rock overlooking what you might say was my former life that I found the last bit of courage to follow through with my pledge to defend the United States of America. It was an important moment for me. I figured I could depend on God, and I shall never forget it. The time was gone and it was nearing evening time with darkness quickly approaching. I left my memories of days gone by and returned to the valley and to my commitment.

December 4 at 7 in the morning, my airplane left Woodrum airport headed for Chicago. Durwood, Hazel, Barbara, Derby and Regina went with me to catch my flight. Mike was not there. They could not walk with me to the airplane but they were standing at the gate. I kissed Barbara goodbye, hugged everyone and walked to the airplane. When I started up the stairs into the airplane, I looked back and waved. I could tell Hazel was crying, but I was unsure about the others. It was a lonesome time for me. I felt the same feelings as when mom died. The stewardess spoke to me as I entered the door and directed me to my seat.

I hoped for a window seat facing the terminal so I could see everyone but it was not to be. I had the window but on the opposite side of the airplane from them, so I sat there waiting to leave. No words can explain my emotions. The stewardess went through her instructions to us and the engines started and soon we were moving. The airplane turned as it pulled off and I could see that no one had left. They were waving to me and I waved back. Oh how I wished I could get off the airplane and not leave. The airplane taxied out to the runway and soon we were in the air.

I looked below at the city. I could see the airport, and I tried to see Durwood's station wagon but could not. I hoped to see my house but that, too, didn't happen. I hoped to see my neighborhood one more time. I remembered what it looked like when flying over it in Hilton's airplane and I really wanted one more look. I did see the Fort Lewis Mountain and my rock, and it offered the comfort I needed at that moment. Soon we flew above the clouds and it was like the world as I knew it was gone.

11

The Trip To Vietnam

My flight landed in Chicago and the stewardess read off the connecting flights. My orders had my flights arranged ahead of time but they depended on seats being available, since I was flying military standby. I had never been in a big airport so I asked her which way to go to catch my next flight. She looked at my ticket and said I only had an hour to make the connection. She said I would have to hurry because my flight was across the terminal. She asked if I was headed for Vietnam and I said "yes." She kissed me on my cheek and wished me, "Good luck!"

It didn't take me long to realize why she said to hurry. The place was massive but I was able to get to the right place, and checked in with the airline clerk. She told me there were no seats on the flight to San Francisco and I would have to wait. In, fact, there were two other military standbys in front of me. It looked like it would be a long stay, but I wasn't too worried because I had plenty of time to report to Travis Air Force Base. I really didn't have to be there until December 8. I thought about asking to have my name removed from the waiting list but decided I would stay in the airport and not venture out into the city of Chicago. I remember looking out of the terminal windows and watching the airplanes coming and going.

It was awesome to realize there was a big world out there that I had not experienced or seen. I found a seat and watched with amazement.

I had just dozed off when I felt the ticket attendant tapping on my shoulder. She said to follow her and she led me to the entrance ramp and wished me well. I was on my way to San Francisco. I never did understand what happened to the two people in front of me. When you fly military standby, it is first come and first served. It was about 1 o'clock in the afternoon. I boarded the plane and took my seat. I hoped my sea bag would follow me since I didn't see it with the other luggage being loaded into the rear of the airplane. Once again, I had a window seat and I could see luggage being loaded into the rear cargo hatch of the airplane.

It was not long before we were in the air. I wondered what the people back home were doing. That seemed to depress me so I involved myself in a magazine that was in the pouch on the back of the seat in front of me. Soon I fell asleep only to be awakened by the stewardess asking if I wanted something to eat. I was hungry so she bought me a chicken dinner and a Coke. We landed at San Francisco airport without any problems. I left the airplane and went to the luggage pick up area. My sea bag was already there. I grabbed it and headed outside the terminal.

It was a shock to me, seeing the busyness of all the things taking place around me. People were hurrying to catch local buses and cab drivers were barking out their services. I was glad I asked the stewardess how to get to Travis. It was just as she said. I looked for the bus stop sign which had 60th Military Airlift Wing, Travis Air Force Base on it. It was not long before a transit bus arrived and I boarded it, paid the fare and sat down for the ride. It felt strange because the time hadn't changed very much since we left Chicago. Boy, was I naive. Of course the time hadn't changed much because we were chasing the sun. The driver let me and several other Marines off at the receiving center at Travis where I reported to the airman on duty.

The Air Force didn't waste any time processing us. The next day we loaded onto a C-130 and were in the air headed for Hickam Air Force Base in Hawaii. There were ten or twelve other Marines with me. That was the Marine Corps practice of sending each Marine with separate orders to Vietnam. We didn't ship out in units. Some traveled through Travis and some through Camp Pendleton.

I will never forget the roughness of flying in a C-130. The seats are no more than jump seats made of canvas and the roar of the engines are deafening. It seemed forever before we landed at Hickam. To our surprise and disappointment we were not allowed to depart the plane. The crew brought us our meal and a drink and said we would be back in the air as soon as they refueled the airplane. I had hoped to spend some time in Hawaii since I had extra time to blow, or at least I thought so. I never dreamed I would be back in Hawaii soon to be treated for wounds.

The crew was right and we were in the air before we finished eating. The next stop would be Da Nang, Vietnam. I will never forget the crew of that C-130. They were easy going until we neared Da Nang. Then things changed dramatically. They came to each one of us and told us that the base was under attack and we were going to land in a hot zone. Panic gripped my thoughts. I suddenly felt my heart pounding inside my chest, and I thought how could this be happening? Just a few days ago I was spending time with my loved ones in Roanoke, Virginia, and now, I was on an airplane getting ready to land in the middle of a Viet Cong (VC) attack, plus I was unarmed. None of the Marine passengers had any weapons to defend ourselves. The crew chief yelled to us our instructions — "Get the hell out of the aircraft as quick as possible when the ramp opens!" I felt the airplane touch down and the engines go into reverse. It practically stood on its nose. The ramp opened and we leaped from the plane. There were military police waiting to lead us to a bunker.

Later, I realized why the pilot stopped the airplane so quickly. The north end of the runway was under a mortar attack and he didn't want to roll into it. I could hear the mortars hitting the base but none of them hit near me or the others in that bunker. Soon it was deathly quiet, and the attack stopped and everyone went about their business. I thought, how strange? I would come to realize that mortar and artillery attacks were a regular happening at Da Nang. You simply learn to deal with it! It was the eighth of December, and I was three days early in arriving.

I remember the smell of the place. It would be typical of the hamlets and villages throughout my stay in Vietnam. It's a smell you cannot forget. There was always a sour rotten garbage odor mingled with wood smoke and human waste. Then there was the animal waste and chicken manure. The tropical heat magnified everything and it was like a sauna. Perspiration and body odor were the norm and there was no way to help it. If you moved, you sweated. Believe it or not, the jungle smelled better than the settled areas, or at least it smelled like mountains and green vegetation, so to speak. This was one aspect of my training that lacked perfection. Thirteen months of this was going to be a challenge.

I reported to the command center and was told I would be trucked to my unit in the morning, located in Phu Bai. I would be joining my unit, Gulf Company, 2nd Battalion, 26th Marines and the 1st Platoon. The first night in Da Nang was a restless one. Gunfire and artillery firing in the distance was just close enough to be a reminder that this place was no war game, and I would be playing for keeps. I laid on my cot thinking about home and puzzled about what would come next until I fell asleep. I am so thankful we don't see the future before it happens!

12

December 1966
An Introduction To Fire

The next morning I loaded onto one of twenty trucks making up the convoy going to Phu Bai. These were six-by-six trucks. We rode up Highway 1 heading north past villages that looked like something out of a fiction book. There were no real houses and the people lived in shacks and worse, grass and sod shelters with thatch or palm leaves for roofs. Occasionally I saw tin used in roof and side construction. Each family compound had shelters for their oxen or buffalo, farm tools, grain storage and the inevitable pig sty or chicken pen. However, it seemed to me that the chickens and pigs roamed loose. Dogs were abundant and always barking. Narrow paths connected the dwellings. Many of the villages had areca palms, guava trees, mango trees, bamboo clumps or banana trees planted to provide some privacy for their houses.

The thing I found most interesting was the way they caught rain water. It was very simple. They placed a tank everywhere there was rain water run-off, mostly under the roof corners. I thought, "These people are from another century. They don't even have running water." Then, of course, there were the filthy smells.

The women squatted instead of sitting and smoked some sort of weed. The children were friendly and waved at us as we passed by them. Soon I would pay them big bucks for a bottle of Coke. Kids would approach us while we were on patrol to sell us Cokes. I thought to myself, what could be so important that we would be fighting for these people? I would quickly learn the answer to that question.

The terrain changed from open vegetative fields, to rice paddies and back to dense jungle that crept in on the road on each side. I saw village men and boys working the land with water buffalos. They were massive animals, and it was impressive to see little boys handling them with no more than switches.

I reported for duty as soon as I arrived. Captain Sam Oots was the Company CO. He greeted me and welcomed me to his company. I liked him immediately. He would prove to be a wise and courageous leader. I also met Second Lieutenant Robert Brown for the first time. He was our Executive Officer and in charge of S2. We would become good friends.

L-R, Cpl. Lyons

They told me that Operation Pawnee was starting that day and they were glad to have me assigned to them. "Your training record is impressive," Captain Oots commented. He introduced me to Corporal "Bones" Lyons, the second squad leader of 1ˢᵗ Platoon, who was also there in the company headquarters. Bones, as we all called him, would give me some very good advice. He was a strikingly tall and lanky Marine, about 180 pounds and all muscle. Corporal Lyons took me to the supply area where I was issued my combat gear — a magazine belt, six magazines of ammunition, a bayonet, a pair of jungle boots and socks, a jungle camouflaged blouse and trousers, a flak jacket, canteen, E-tool, nap sack, poncho, shelter half, a helmet and my M-14 rifle. I still remember my rifle serial number, 634282.

Bones liked me and on the walk back to our area he told me there were only a few things to remember. He said, "Don't ask your men to do something you wouldn't do." He said, "If you can, do it yourself." I asked, "Like what?" He said, "Like disarming booby traps." He continued, "Don't play favorites and don't make friends. Take the time to get to know your men." Then he chuckled, "And keep your head down." I liked him immediately. He showed me to my squad hootch, which was a large tent placed on a wooden floor with a sand bag bunker in front of it, and he was on his way.

L-R, Horrell, Ayers, Frye

I felt odd walking into the presence of fourteen Marines that I had never met, but it was time to introduce myself to them. I met and shook each one's hand; Corporal Hall, Private First Class Frye, Private First Class Holdgrafer, Private First Class Manning. They would be my first fire team. My second fire team was Lance Corporal Aguon, Private First Class Cox, Private First Class Cahalane, and Private First Class Powers. The third fire team was Lance Corporal Miller, Lance Corporal Johnson, Private First Class Marshall and Private First Class Moore. My M-79 man was Private First Class Horrell. Lance Corporal Sewell was my radio man. Pfc. Frye and Pfc. Cahalane would on occasion carry the radio.

L-R, Miller, Cox, Marshall, Holdgraher, Aguon, Powers

103

Their dress caught my attention immediately. Their boots were worn and bleached and their uniforms were ragged and faded. I would learn very quickly that I could not wear underwear. It only resulted in a diaper rash effect from the chaffing. The extreme heat, always like a sauna, caused your clothes to stick to you like glue. I stood out like a sore thumb with all new equipment and clothes but it wouldn't be long before I fit right in.

Several of us would become very close — Aguon, Cahalane, Marshall, Horrell, Frye and Johnson. These were good Marines and everyone would show bravery beyond what could be told in the pages of a book. I grew to depend on and honor each of them. They were not sure what to make of me at first. I was the new guy on the scene and unproved under fire. It was a normal reaction for anyone to express. That first meeting reflected their cautiousness toward me, and the talk was limited so I decided to leave them to themselves to process what just had happened.

I decided to go down to where Bones and some other Marines were sitting on top of a bunker, after I introduced myself to my new squad. Bones introduced me to several of his men. I had just sat down with them when they were gone in a flash. They heard what I didn't hear, a sniper shot. One of them pulled me off the top of the bunker and I fell on top of him. "You idiot," he exclaimed as he pushed me off of him. "Did you hear that shot?" I think they all thought I was deaf or stupid. It was my first exposure to fire and I had not reacted properly.

I learned they had been exposed to sniper fire constantly since December 1 and were much attuned to sniper fire. The Viet Cong were very active in the area. In fact, lights shining after dark in the local villages could be seen and that was a direct hint of VC movement. The innocent villagers knew not to use lights during that time even though occasionally they would forget. Contact with the VC had been regular. Our company had killed eight VC in the last several weeks. Bones' squad had captured several VC while in ambush and on patrols between December 1 and 9. They were turned over to district headquarters.

Just before my arrival on December 8 'Gulf' Company had contact with six Viet Cong, and killed one of them later that afternoon and spotted seven more on a ridgeline just ahead of them. One VC was killed when the company engaged them in a firefight. The same action would plague us during the rest of December. Our mission remained controlling the Lang Co Bridge area and denying the VC access to Highway 1 and the local railroad.

There was no real contact made with the Viet Cong from December 11, when I arrived, until December 15 when one VC was captured by one of our patrols. The same day one of our squads acting in support of a Logistical Support Activity team was fired upon. They returned the fire and killed three VC who were attempting to escape the area in a small boat. Later that day four more VC insurgents were killed. Things settled down until December 18.

A runner from our command post came and got me on the evening of December 18. He told me to report to the CP immediately. Staff Sergeant Perez was waiting for me. I knew I had a mission since it was my rotation to go out. He also said movement had been reported down by the Song Phu River and that flashing lights had been spotted moving in the vicinity of a village near our base camp. He wanted me to take my squad and investigate it. He ordered me to return fire only if we were fired upon first and if we could identify the target.

This was my first real test as a squad leader. I had led a few day time patrols but nothing like this. I hoped I would be up to whatever happened, and I must say I was very nervous, but I had to hide that from my men. They must not see any fear in me. I was probably too forceful in explaining our patrol objective to them because of this. My squad, who was already on standby, was nearly ready to proceed. We painted our face, camouflaged ourselves, and checked our gear. I handed out 100 rounds of ammo and several grenades to each of them, and we left the perimeter at 2030 hours.

The intelligence was correct. There were lights in the village not far from our position. I could see them moving around. Probably those lights were a sign of Viet Cong movement. The village was not in view for most of our approach. Therefore I slowed our pace to a crawl. The VC insurgents were good at luring the enemy into a trap. We saw no lights or movement within the hamlets once we were within a hundred meters of the village's main entrance. I stopped our advance and called for my fire team leaders to meet with me, and I laid out our plan of approach. I told our radio man to put the radio on squelch. We approached the village through several openings near the main entrance.

We crossed a road and entered a path that had some brush on each side and boarded the Song Phu River. The path ended and there was a small opening between it and the village dwellings. The village was run down and the hamlets were spread out, not close to one another as usual. Visibility was good even though it was night time.

Barking dogs had announced our arrival, so we didn't have the advantage of surprise. I decided to move forward into the opening but with more distance than normal between each of us. My squad did exactly what we had talked about if we took fire from within the village. Dennis Johnson was walking point with his fire team following directly behind him. They were spaced five or six meters apart and the rest of us followed twenty or so meters behind them. We were fired on by an unknown number of Viet Cong. The fire was sporadic; not consistent with a large number of VC soldiers.

The first VC shot went through Johnson's trousers, just missing his leg. Maybe fifteen or twenty other rounds hit the dirt around him. He dropped to the ground and returned fire immediately while his team moved up and took up positions on each side of him. My other two fire teams and I moved into the opening to the right side. There was no other enemy fire, but we spotted four VC fighters leaving the back of a dwelling. We fired upon them, and I am not sure if we hit any of them. We had good coverage so I waited for several minutes. Our hearts were pounding and the adrenaline was high. I motioned for us to move closer to the dwellings. We moved slowly, ready to fire at any sign of VC, but we received no more enemy fire.

We took up circular position facing the remaining hamlets where no sign of movement was present. None of the villagers was talking which is a sure sign that more VC were nearby. I made the decision to not search the entire village, and we back tracked ourselves and returned home. It was my introduction to real action. I believe that night my squad began to trust my ability to take care of them. I was thankful no more Viet Cong wanted to fight that night. Four were enough!

The same situation happened on the December 23. We were on a company patrol along the same river south of Phu Bai. It was in support of a new operation, code name Chinook, and our company was on a search-and-destroy mission at night. It was always risky to patrol at night in a company size-mission. Our point saw lights on the river and called for the CO. He ordered a squad to proceed with caution and investigate the situation. Bones took his squad and moved forward to the river bank, and were fired on by several VC insurgents. The firefight ended with one VC killed. He fell in the river and floated past the squad. It wasn't a pretty site. One VC was wounded and the others fled in a northwest direction.

Ambush patrols were much different than regular day patrols. I will never forget my first ambush. On December 30 our platoon started a search and destroy mission. The main purpose was to set two night ambushes and my squad was to carry out one of those ambushes. We left the patrol base at 1900 hours and moved about a mile from that position, and set up in some dense brush beside a narrow dirt road leading into Thon My Luvng. The road ran north of the village, and reports stated that the VC used it at night to transport supplies into their positions in the area. My squad had settled in for the night. There was to be no noise of any kind and no talking. The radio was on squelch. Every hour the CP would signal us by giving three short squelches and we would reply by returning two. I would initiate the ambush by firing first, then everyone else was to fire twenty rounds into the ambush sight, more if absolutely necessary.

I was in my position in the brush beside the road when I felt a stinging feeling on my neck. I felt my neck and realized it was cover with leeches. It was terrifying. There were too many of them to ignore. I had to remove them without disturbing the ambush silence. I had forgotten to put my bug repellent on. I was able to reach it in my trouser pocket and carefully sprayed it on my neck and every other body part that was exposed, and they turned lose. It was a long night.

We departed the ambush the next morning at 0800 hours and returned to the patrol base. That morning I had more than twenty leeches attached to me. I was horrified, to say the least. Several others had the same problem.

Leeches were not the only challenges we faced; there were poisonous snakes, rats, tigers, mosquitoes, bees and wild pigs, just to mention a few.

During the latter part of December our battalion, along with Foxtrot Company, Hotel Company and Echo Company, was linked up with 3rd Battalion 26th Marines in Operation Chinook. Operation Pawnee had finished. My company, Gulf Company, was helicoptered from Phu Bai to our positions in and around Phu Loc on December 24 where we ran night ambushes and day patrols into the villages of Cho Cau Hai, Thon Vong Tri and Thon Loa Luong. We were assigned to 2nd Battalion 9th Marines during this short time span. We, also, acted as support for truck convoys that ran along the coast between Phu Loc and Luong Dien.

Christmas Eve seemed to be especially hard for me, but I think it was hard on all of us being away from our loved ones. Christmas had always been my favorite holiday. I remember reading the Bible that Hazel gave me the night before I left home to come to this place. I tried to understand it but nothing really made any sense to me, so I laid down on my make-shift cot and let my mind wander back through the many Christmas times at home. I thought about my first bicycle. That was probably the best Christmas I ever had. I received a Schwinn. It came with fenders and a horn built into its side panel, and I shall never forget seeing it beside the Christmas tree. The smell of white pine and the lights of the tree reflecting on that new shiny bike were magnificent. Then I thought about what Barbara and her family were doing and I wonder if they were thinking about me. I thought about Mike and wished I could share the night with all of them. Wishful thinking didn't ease the lonesomeness. Several of us gathered together and we sang as many Christmas songs as we could remember. I think we changed the verses of some of them. None of us got much sleep that night longing for home.

I spent Christmas Day preparing for Operation Chinook, but mostly I just sat around doing nothing. We were still in a defensive posture. That operation was conducted mostly by 3rd Battalion 26th Marines, and our battalion was in support of them. The weather was miserable and didn't allow for too much activity. The rain fell in buckets, and staying dry was a challenge. The temperature would climb to the 70's during the day and drop to the 50's at night.

Immersion foot and respiratory problems were dominant. I remember my feet were raw in places and it hurt to put my socks on. Can you imagine what it was like to wear combat boots? But we did what we had to do. Some of our men had to wait for their foot problems to heal enough for them to walk safely, so the rest of us covered for them. The weather was especially hard on us because our company was mobile. We had no fixed patrol bases from which we were operating which meant we couldn't make any sort of permanent shelter in order to stay dry.

13

January 1966
My First Real Test

The month of January was split into two halves for us. We spent January 1 through January 14 in the Phu Loc area. My company was choppered back to Phu Bai between January 15 and January 19 where we basically rested. Then between January 21 and January 23 we went to Hill 724 outside of Da Nang, while the other three companies went to Da Nang, a company at a time, and relieved the 3rd Battalion 7th Marines in the northwest sector of Da Nang. Their mission was to secure the area. They conducted numerous day patrols and night ambushes.

It was not a good month for some of my comrades. We lost three Marines and one officer due to enemy fire, mostly from snipers. Five men were wounded and several suffered from heat exhaustion. My squad was fortunate. We didn't lose anyone during this time, and I was very thankful for that. The men in my squad were good Marines, and I had grown to respect each of their abilities. We were a darn good fighting unit and in several months we would prove it.

Our platoon settled in, and we started going on regular patrols and ambushes. The contact was moderate. Bones and his squad located a 60-mm round booby trap that was placed just two feet off the path. He blew it in place with C-4. Sergeant Hellet, the third squad leader, found his squad in a mess when they were fired upon while returning back to our base camp by one of our outposts, but none of his squad was hit. They sure were unhappy about the entire incident. My squad found a TNT booby trap on January 26 around 0920 hours.

Aguon was walking point that morning. He had a good nose for booby traps, and he had saved our bacon many times already. Our patrol started in the dense brush of the mountainous area around our base camp and was to move to the lower valley where there was a village, Cau Trang, and a stream. The plan was to patrol Highway 1 back to our base camp.

Soon into our mission, about 1100 hours, Aguon spotted a one-pound block of TNT about three feet off of the trail. Naturally he froze in place and hand signaled me to come forward, which I did. That was our common procedure. He pointed into the thicket to the booby trap that looked unusual, it had no trip wire. Usually the detonator was near the booby trap, a wire stretched across the path or an electric contact placed under the foliage on the path. Instead there were two wires attached to the TNT block that led into the bush, and that caused me to be very alarmed. Either it was a set up for an ambush and possibly more booby traps just off the trail, or we were being watched by the VC who could set it off at their choosing. Either possibility was not a good situation for my squad.

I passed the word for Johnson, who had become my right hand man, to come forward. I ordered him to move the squad back down the trail to a safe position, and told him to have every other man watch each side of the path and to get very low to the ground. I left Johnson in control, and Aguon and I followed the wire. It wasn't easy and we were more than cautious. The wires followed a very narrow path, not wide enough to walk untouched by the brush on each side of it. It was something like a deer path back home except the brush was thicker and overhung the path in many places. It required Aguon to move it to the side in several places. It was nearly impossible to move quietly, but we tried. Our readiness was high and our movement guarded, and we heard and saw everything that moved.

I had learned in my training that this was one of the most dangerous booby traps. They were setup to detonate without the VC having to engage us. We moved farther and farther into the bush, and soon our squad was out of our sight. We moved nearly 600 feet off the trail before we found the detonator, an old radio battery. One wire was attached to the battery's positive terminal and one was tied to a stick in the ground beside it. Aguon and I studied the surroundings carefully.

I ordered Aguon to move back down the way we came in the exact same steps or as close as possible. He moved about fifty feet away and refused to go any farther. He was a good Marine, and determined not to leave me alone. I learned in training to never see only the obvious when dealing with booby traps. I took my bayonet and probed the ground in front of me as I approached the battery. The last thing I wanted was to set off an anti-personal mine. I figured the battery was sitting on another trap, so I was careful not to move it in the least. I probed around and under it very carefully with my bayonet. It hit nothing solid and so I felt fairly confident that no other devices were hooked to it. I knew no other booby traps were hooked to the wires because we were careful to watch for that possibility when we followed them to this battery. So I removed the wire from the battery.

113

Probing for booby trap

Now I needed to remove the stick. It could be holding a device in place under the ground that would detonate a booby trap in a different location. In other words, the TNT could be a decoy requiring me to probe around it as gently as possible. I determined there were no other mines. Now it was time to remove the stick and battery. The sweat was streaming off of me even though I had checked them carefully. I decided to remove the stick first. My heart was pounding, but everything around me seemed to be deathly silent. My hands were unsteady, but I slowly lifted the stick straight up hoping I heard no clicks from another trap under it. Everything was safe with the stick, so I slowly lifted the battery. No explosions, thank goodness. We took the battery and back-tracked to the location of the TNT.

I radioed the command post and explained our situation and asked permission to blow the TNT. They gave the go ahead. Johnson had rejoined us to check our situation. The process started all over again. I told Johnson to keep the squad back down the trail from which we had come, and he did just that. I forced Aguon to go with Johnson. Once they were out of range of an explosion, I probed the TNT block much the same way I had done the battery. The VC hadn't added any surprises, so I carefully laid the battery beside the TNT block; and placed a quarter pound of C-4 beside the TNT and placed a blasting cap in it. I attached the fuse wires to it and unraveled them as I made my way to the squad. I hooked the wires to the detonator and set off the C-4, which exploded the TNT. All was well, and we continued the patrol down the mountain toward Binh Lien Chieu, our next check point located in the valley.

Aguon was still walking point when we neared an opening into a dried field near the hamlet. It was hot and everyone was tired, and our nerves were on edge. Our water was low, and our feet were killing us, so I stopped the patrol for a needed break. There for a moment it seemed like any other day. We could see a boy crossing a stream of water with his water buffalo. I couldn't really see all that he was doing, but it didn't make any difference. We rested for several minutes.

I decided to move Powers to the point position for some needed experience since I didn't foresee any problems. I told him to lead us around the edge of the field. I didn't want us exposed in the open in case any Viet Cong were in the hamlet. Everything was fine until he neared the stream, but for some unknown reason, the water buffalo that we had watched a few minutes earlier charged Powers. He reacted the same way anyone would have reacted. He shot it five times, killing it.

The chieftain of the hamlet was very upset and things became really hectic. These animals were not only their livelihood but also their pets. The little boy was crying and the other villagers were gathered around trying to console him. I sensed the situation was going to get out of hand. My squad was on edge. I radioed the command post for instructions, and

115

was ordered to tell the chieftain that the Marines would replace the animal and that we were very sorry. I was also told to get away from the village quickly and return to our base camp. It was almost impossible to explain to the old man what we would do for them, especially since Jim, our Vietnamese interpreter was not with us. None of us was fluent in Vietnamese. Finally, he seemed to understand. It was about 1300 hours, and we were at least three hours from home.

Doc Turner – taking a break

I picked a direct route back to Highway 1 from the hamlet, and we came upon it in about thirty minutes. It had been a hectic day, and the walk back up the road to the camp was long and tiring. I thought to myself, "Of all things that could happen to a bunch of Marines, we would have to shoot a water buffalo — not the VC, but a water buffalo. How in the world was I going to explain this to the platoon leader, especially when we were trying to build our relationship with the locals?" But the longer we climbed Highway 1, the funnier it became. We reached the base camp totally exhausted at about 1600 hours.

My meeting with the Company XO, 2nd Lieutenant Robert Brown, was anything but humorous. My platoon leader took me to speak with him, and I think he may have had a butt chewing by our CO before I arrived. Brown had a way of letting a person know when he wasn't happy, and to say the least he wasn't pleased with me. He wanted to know what happened and I told him. He asked, "If I would have shot the animal and I told him, "Absolutely! It was either the water buffalo or Pfc. Powers." Strangely, that began a good relationship between Brown and me.

That night I woke up in a cold sweat. My dreams were all over the place, from bombs exploding to water buffalos charging. I thought, "What if the trap had exploded or there had been VC waiting to spring an ambush? Why did I put an inexperienced man up front? He could have been killed! Did I do the right thing? Did I make the right call? My platoon sergeant was happy with the results, but was I? This time things worked out alright, but would it be the same next time?" Finally, utter exhaustion took over and I fell asleep. Hopefully the next day would be better.

I took out three more patrols between January 29 and January 31. We had no luck engaging the VC. Bones' luck was not much better. He had several of his squad members medevac'd because of heat strokes. Meanwhile, Sergeant Heller's third squad set off an ambush on a bridge but managed to kill no VC. They thought they hit several gooks but couldn't find the bodies; and to make things worse, my squad was surprised by a VC crossing a road in front of us. We missed him when we finally took the shot. The month ended on a down note.

14

February 1967
The Reason I Fight

View from Hill 724

The month of February still found us on Hill 724 serving as a guard unit for the (LAM) Missile Support Base. The view from on top of Hill 724 was beautiful. You could see some of Highway 1, a village, Go Lien Chieu, and the South China Sea in the far distance. Sometimes I forgot I was in a war. It reminded me so much of the mountains back home, especially the view from my rock, but watching "Puff the Magic Dragon" changed that idea quickly. "Puff", as we called it, was an old

C-47 propelled driven airplane which has three electric Gatling guns, known as Vulcans, mounted on the left side of the airplane.

The pilots would fly it with the left side pointing down to the ground while firing the guns. One out of every five rounds fired was a tracer, which caused a red laser type of light. It fired so fast that the stream of bullets appeared as one solid red line; and it was deadly, and the VC hated it. It could cover an area of a football field with one round every square foot in about five seconds, and nothing caught in its field of fire lived to tell about it!

Our squads still ran regular day patrols and night ambushes, as the weather permitted. Some of these patrols reached as far as the Song De River Valley. The nice thing about this base on Hill 724 was the showing of flicks (movies) and an NCO club where beer was served to off duty Marines. I didn't go to the club. Somehow I felt this would violate my deal with God, plus I had sworn that I would never touch the stuff because of my father's behavior. However, many of my squad members enjoyed themselves and that was alright with me. They deserved a break from patrols when it came.

Base camp – Hill 724

When we were not on patrol, we were building bunkers, filling sand bags or playing poker, testing our rifles and cleaning our gear which was an everyday job. Chow time wasn't that great. It was either cooked food or C-rations and both were awful. Everyone thought I was strange because I would exchange the good stuff for lima beans, but I loved them and was known as a pack rat. Occasionally there was a cat nap in order, if you could find a decent breeze and some shade.

I did have a problem with the Marines taking advantage of the young girls that came with their fathers to do our laundry. The fathers would sell their daughters to us for sexual favors. I didn't take part in this and I voiced my opinion with 2nd Lt. Brown who didn't approve but he looked away when it happened. I realize it was war time, but many of those girls were just kids. It wasn't a large number of men who took advantage of the girls, but the ones who did disliked my objections. They knew I was not a saint. Many nights I played poker with them until sunup. They considered gambling to be as evil as prostitution. I didn't!

We had no major operations in February but we did receive sniper fire and fourteen attempts by the VC to penetrate our perimeter which was not an easy task for them. We had several rows of barbed wire and concertina wire encircling the entire perimeter. The wire was staked to the ground and extended about chest high, and we set anti-personal mines between the rows of wire. We hung empty tin cans on the wire that would make noise when the wire moved making a primitive alarm system, but it worked. The Viet Cong were always setting booby traps. They were the VC's main source of harassing us.

There was one night that turned out to be humorous. There was a family of Rock Apes that lived outside the perimeter. They got their name because they would throw rocks at us during the night. The rocks would hit the wire and make us think the VC were throwing hand grenades at us.

They were mostly tree dwellers but on occasion they would attempt to slip into our perimeter. I suppose they were looking for food.

Anyway, on this one well-lit evening, several tried to get past me and Cox. We were standing guard in one of the outer bunkers. Durwood had mailed me a.32 caliber pistol to carry as a side arm, and I needed a chance to see if it would actually stop a person, so I decided to shoot one of the rock apes. He must have sensed his danger because he turned and ran when I aimed at him. He was in between the two rows of wire, about thirty meters from me, when I took the shot. I hit him in his butt. He grabbed his tail and sprang over the outside wire landing on the other side, got up and stared at me for the longest time. He made a screeching call and headed for the trees. I thought Cox would die from laughter. "Oh yes, the VC will love that thing!" He snickered referring to the pistol in my hand.

Early in the month, on February 4 and 5, my squad along with Bone's squad went on a two-day patrol and ambush mission near Nui Hoi in the area of Hill 1100. Hill 1100 was about two miles from our base camp on Hill 724 and in heavy mountainous terrain. Bones' squad led the way to our objective, and the climb was slow and tiring. Once there we set up our outpost some fifty yards from the perimeter. That first night we sent out two ambush patrols. There was no movement by the VC, so we broke camp the next day around 1100 hours and returned to our position on Hill 724 at about 1400 hours. Bones and I were disappointed because the day before, our 3rd squad had made contact with the VC and lost one Marine who was wounded by friendly fire. We thought we might make contact with some reported movement of Viet Cong in that area, but it didn't happen, and our request to extend the patrol was refused by the CP. We had to return in order to train on the M-16 rifles that were arriving. We learned that Pfc. Meloin Moffett was killed in a firefight in a different location.

The next day was spent learning the nomenclature of the M-16 rifle and the many problems with it. We fired it, and I wasn't impressed at all with it. It jammed on more than one occasion with me. None of my men really liked it, but as usual, we would not have a choice in the decision to change over to it from the M-14. It did have one advantage since it was lighter than the M-14, but the M-14 was a more dependable rifle. Another problem was the automatic fire selector on the rifle which meant it could be used as a single fire semi-automatic or a fully automatic weapon. This would prove to be a problem in fire fights when everyone wanted to use the fully automatic option. The ammunition would be used up too quickly in a firefight, and it became a real problem when we encountered the North Vietnamese Regular Army in May.

I guess the most embarrassing thing that happened to me in Vietnam took place on February 14. I took my squad and a gun team on patrol into the mountainous terrain to the right of Highway 1. Our objective was to search for VC movement in the pass at the foot of Hill 1192 and then follow the stream to where it forked with another stream at the foot of Hill 600. We were to return by the same route. It sounded like a simple mission, but a problem occurred.

The problem that occurred was twofold. First, my compass did not give accurate directions, and second, our radio failed. We found the pass and searched for any signs of VC movement and found none. We also found the head of the stream that we were to follow to Hill 600, but that was where I ran into trouble. We never did cross another stream of water that joined it. The map showed another stream but it wasn't there, and we ended up on a trail that led us down to Hill 100.

I decided to cut across the terrain in an attempt to find Highway 1. The severity of the terrain was less challenging and the mountain slopes were not nearly as steep. Finally, I heard the noise from vehicles and we followed the sounds to the highway. We intersected Highway 1 just above the village of Hon So Mu, but we were past due getting back and without radio contact, the CP was very uneasy.

It wasn't easy but I decided we would force-march six miles back to our CP. The highway was uphill the entire way to our base camp. The men were tired, discouraged, confused and very upset with me, but they did what Marines do, they got the job done. I couldn't blame them because I was just as angry over the affair. My squad and the fact that the radio went out on us saved my hide that day. My CO accepted my explanation of the events of the day.

Football game

The long days on Hill 724 were broken up by some good times of competition. Someone received a football one day in the mail, and that opened up a great time of team playing. I had two very gifted players in my squad, Pfc. Horrell who played fullback for Iowa State and Pfc. Frye who played tail back for Southern Methodist University. Obviously my squad had the advantage over the challengers. It was good to hold a football in my hand, and I loved every minute of those times playing.

We didn't have much of a football field to play on, but we made the best of it. There were several spirited games while we were assigned to Hill 724, and I must admit that I really felt homesick during that time. After all, I would be playing high school football, if I had stayed home like Hazel had begged me to do, and probably dating and having the time of my life. But I chose my path and now I was living it even though it wasn't the easiest choice; but I had a sense of pride, a Marine family and I knew I was doing something special and much bigger than me.

I guess this is a good place to explain my understanding of Vietnam, or why we were here fighting. I said earlier that it seemed confusing to be so far away from the United States and to be fighting an enemy that couldn't destroy us, like Japan or Germany of World War II, but over the last weeks

I had changed my opinion. Interacting with the people had influenced my thinking. Many of our patrols were conducted as good will missions, so I got to see many things. I watched the children play games on barren dirt roads and on paths, and I watched them work all day in the hot sun or in a driving rain storm so that they would have food to eat. Once I watched a boy chase a chicken until he caught it so his mother could cook it for supper. I had done the same thing on the farm. I watched a kid who had lost a leg in a bobby trap meant for us, playing on a dirt road, and so I felt for the kids.

I saw their mothers and fathers care for them as much as most American parents. I felt for them as they begged food from us while we would be on patrol in their villages. There were a few times when Mike and I went hungry, so I felt for these people. They were everyday people trying to make the best of what life had dealt them. It was just that they were stuck in overwhelming poverty and that touched my heart for them.

Freedom became a big issue for me personally. They deserved to be free. I could relate to that virtue, because I always rebelled against the thought of anyone taking my freedom away. I imagined an enemy aggressor in our beloved homeland and realized evil must be stopped where it is! I learned from watching the results of war that freedom isn't free—someone must defend it, either here in Vietnam or some other place. The majority of these people wanted to be free. It is true they were backward and simple people but they deserved to live in peace.

I also saw what was done to many of them by the VC insurgents when they didn't want to fight for them. My squad arrived in one hamlet about two days too late to stop many acts of butchery. I witnessed fathers who had their tongues cut out, fingers or an arm cut off because they refused to

125

give up their children to the VC fighters. The gooks were not beyond muti-lating bodies to prove their point. I saw women with their eyes blinded because they spoke to us. One time, when I was in an outpost at night, I heard the cries for help when the VC came into a nearby village, raped the women and dragged off their young ones to be forced to fight for a cause they didn't understand. I saw the carnage left behind after the VC rum-maged a village that supported us. I heard their cries and mourning over the death of their loved ones and I hurt with them as they tried to break the language barrier in expression of their pain to us. One day I thought, "They hurt just like we do when we lose a loved one."

These people lived hell on this Earth. I am not sure why the other Marines fought in Vietnam, but I fought for their chance at freedom. I've heard the stories of how we killed innocent babies and children and were drug addicts. Well, I am telling you that I was there and those stories weren't true of us. It was the gooks killing the innocent, and I will tell you, I didn't mind killing as many of them as I could.

Mail call for me wasn't something I looked forward to because I very seldom received any news from home. I got used to not hearing my name called as the mail was being passed out, so when I did receive a letter it was special. Hazel was the only regular and faithful one to write to me. She was an angel, and good to send me all the latest news about the foot-ball team at Andrew Lewis. She included newspaper clippings of the team and, occasionally would send articles about the war. Those articles were depressing to me and they were not flattering at all. They very seldom had anything good to say about what we were accomplishing. Sometimes Bar-bara would include a note or Hazel would tell me about her day, and that was nice. Hazel always ended her letters by reminding me that she was praying for me and my friends. I think her prayers put a protective shield around me.

I did receive a couple of letters from Dr. Brown. Esther was a nice woman and thought our cause was a good one. I remember enjoying listening to the other men talking about their girlfriends or wives, and we all loved it when one of them sent a care package. That usually meant we would share in the goodies — cookies, chewing gum and whatever. Hazel sent me a large box of chocolate chip cookies once. They were gooey from the heat and the box was crushed but it had come nearly 11,000 miles, too. The cookies only lasted about ten minutes. I guess we were lucky in the mail department because not one of us got a "dear John letter."

February would be a costly mouth for 2/26. We lost several Marines from other platoons; L/Cpl. Glenn Harris was killed by a booby trap, and L/Cpl. George Jeffries was killed in a mortar attack. Chaplain Lt. Bob Brett, Sergeant Billy McCall, L/Cpl. Julius Foster, Pfc. David Cramer, Pfc. Hector Semidey and Pfc. Al Chin were killed by mortar fire, as they attended a Catholic Mass.

15

March 1967
My First Major Firefight

My battalion would be engaged in three operations in March: Operations Prairie II and III and Gulf. The month would be remembered for high temperatures, little drinking water and several serious encounters with the enemy. We remained in Da Nang from March 1 until March 7. We lost one Marine during that period, L/Cpl. Charles Bricker and Cpl. Ray Aldridge. Ray and I had just met. We moved to Dong Ha on March 8.

My squad, along with Sgt. Hallet's 3rd squad, conducted an area-wide sweep north of our base camp near the village of Goi Lang Co. We were trucked into the area where Viet Cong movement had been reported. It was my birthday, March 2, and not the way I had hoped to spend it. No birthday cake on this day. I was nineteen-years-old. It was hot and not the best of situations for a sweeping action with the terrain being mostly open, and subjected us to an easy ambush by the Viet Cong. Sergeant Hallet spotted a good number of boats near the inlet of a stream empting into the Loc Hai Channel, and they appeared to be unloading some sort of supplies. His squad arrived late in the area and nothing was found. There was no contact made with the VC, but we were ordered to remain in the area that night, so we set up a perimeter and security outposts. No ambushes were sent out, and we returned to our base camp by noon the next day and were trucked back to the main battalion.

My battalion was moved by truck from Hill 724 to Da Nang where we were flown to Dong Ha. We landed in Dong Ha and immediately boarded trucks and went to Camp Carroll. The next day my company, Gulf Company, moved north toward the DMZ. This was the start of Prairie II. I was uneasy about the suddenness of the moves which usually meant there were reliable reports of enemy activity. In fact, there were reports of thirty-six VC insurgents operating in the villages from Thon Bang Son to Thon Thien Xuan. These reports came from informants within the villages.

Our orders were to patrol these areas, set up listening posts, and report any movement to headquarters. My squad conducted one of the patrols to carry out this mission. We moved into the area, and I deployed my three fire teams in positions some seventy-five meters apart and several hundred meters outside the village of Thon Bang Son.

The terrain was mostly open but had small clumps of brush spread out in front of our positions. Sometimes the night can cause you to see things or imagine things that are not there and this was one of those nights. One of my fire teams, led by Johnson, radioed me that they were seeing movement. I carefully worked my way to them. They were dug in at the opening into a field with bushes growing throughout the field, maybe seventy-five meters out. They said the bushes were moving. I stared out into the field trying to see what they were seeing. It reminded me of hunting deer back home and the many times I watched a field just before day-break trying to see the movement of deer. Many times I thought I saw deer when I didn't, and this was the same, the more I stared the more it seemed they were right. Now what? Should we report movement and call in illumination?

It was just dark enough that I couldn't get a fix on something beyond the brush to compare its location. Swift moving clouds hid the moon enough to make it impossible to be absolutely sure. I felt the agonizing pressure of the moment. If those bushes were moving it very well could be the VC moving in closer to attack our main unit. I knew the Viet Cong were around the area because of repeated reports of newly set booby trap a few days earlier. If the bushes were not moving, it was our imagination. I decided to wait, and as morning came, there was nothing there but brush. Vietnam had claimed another sleepless night!

Things seemed to be intensifying. We heard that Company Hotel had found a one week old bivouac area that covered over 500 meters, large enough to accommodate a battalion of NVA soldiers. That was cause for great concern because the Viet Cong fighters didn't occupy large bivouacs; instead they operated in small bands of fighters. It seems that the Viet Cong and the NVA were working together in the area. The face of our enemy was about to change.

All of our units were being harassed by small arms and mortar fire but the enemy didn't seem to want to fight us one-on-one. Our artillery support located in Gio Linh, B Battery, 2nd Battalion 94th Artillery, was being pounded by the NVA gunners that confirmed we were dealing with larger fighting units. They received 750 rounds in seven attacks on March 1 and 2, and they were bombarded with mortars and artillery for the next two weeks. They received 927 incoming rounds from 105-mm and 152-mm artillery cannons and 122-mm rockets on March 20 alone, but they withstood the assaults and hammered back at the NVA position in the DMZ. There sure seemed to be a big battle forming on the horizon.

Our 3rd Platoon started receiving sniper fire on March 12 and they lost one Marine, Pfc. Roosevelt Scott from Florida, due to one of our own artillery rounds falling short of its target. That was always a damning thing to us. It was one thing to die while fighting the enemy, but a wasteful thing to die by a mishap. It left us with a feeling of burning hatred inside for the enemy, even more so than normal.

Jim and Ayers

I will never forget one patrol. It stands out in my mind, and took place on March 12. I had Jim, our Vietnamese interpreter, with me. Jim was a very young sixteen-year-old boy. We didn't know if he was an orphan and knew nothing of his background. Some said his parents were murdered by the VC, but one thing we knew for sure, he hated the Viet Cong and anyone who supported them.

Our mission was to gather information about VC involvement in and around a particular village, Thon An Hung, which was sympathetic to the VC

131

cause. Jim had gone into the chieftain's dwelling to speak with a mama's son, and insisted on being alone with her. He believed she had information that she wasn't telling us. We knew she had lost her husband due to the fighting in the local area. The rest of us were outside the dwelling in defensive positions, listening and watching for any Viet Cong.

I could hear Jim tell her, "Lai day" or "come here". She screamed, "Caca dau!" That meant in English, "I'll kill you!" All I could hear then was Jim saying, "Con biet?" "Do you understand?" He said it several times. Suddenly a shot rang out. I rushed into the dwelling ready to engage the VC but instead found the woman lying in her own blood. She had been shot in the side of her head. Jim claimed he was shooting at a VC who rose up out of a spider hole behind her and he missed him but hit her. We never knew for sure because there was a spider hole in the dwelling and it was behind her. Nevertheless, she was dead and we got no information from anyone else. We were ordered to leave the body behind which was unusual because we normally had to bring the dead back to camp. It was kept quiet, not much talk about it, and all Jim would say is that she was very bad.

Dead VC

Our company and Hotel Company were ordered to the north to search for NVA units, and my squad was ordered to an objective, the Song Con Do area, where known VC had operated in and around. There were many trails in this area and the NVA were using them to their advantage. Our mission was to stop that privilege. Unfortunately, we didn't find any NVA, but Hotel Company was ambushed, losing one Marine, L/Cpl. Tim Cox.

It wasn't a total wash, however. Our companies found a tunnel measuring ten feet deep and running towards the north. It had no dirt at the opening and no camouflage, which caused us to think it had just been dug. It was blown with C-4. The enemy would have to try another approach. It reminded me of a cat and mouse game. We were looking for a fight and they were avoiding us, but why? It was obvious they had a large fighting army dodging us. Why were they not willing to fight us? I am afraid some of us, me included, started to think they were afraid of a fight. We would be proven wrong soon enough! They were preparing a detailed attack that would test our will to fight.

During Prairie III, a few days later on March 18, our platoon engaged the VC in a firefight with several snipers. Bones almost met his maker that day when a sniper intended to shoot him in the back of his head, but instead the bullet hit his helmet knocking it off of his head. Other than a headache, Bones was not wounded. The thing that impressed me about Bones was his professionalism at the time. He was strictly about business and kept his squad focused on the mission before them. When the talk got back to me about what had happened, I was panicked. He could have been killed and there was nothing I could have done about it. He was my friend, and my anger seethed within me. I saw him some time later and said, "Bones, you need to keep your head down, remember?" He just smiled with an uneasy expression. Our mental toughness was being tested.

Boarding CH-46's

Our company was choppered in CH-46's to the Rock Pile and Razor Back on March 18 to relieve the 3rd Battalion 3rd Marines. Both Operations Prairie II and III would take place in this area. Our platoon would be a blocking force to stop the VC from retreating into the DMZ. Prairie II would prove to be difficult for our platoon as we would have several intense firefights involving small arms and machine gun fire.

My first real encounter with a major firefight took place at this time. My squad was sweeping an area of downed trees and sage-brush when we came under a hail of bullets from an enemy position to our right flank. Bones had his squad to our left and couldn't return fire without taking a chance of hitting us, and Hallet was behind us with his squad. We hit the ground and returned the fire.

The bullets were hitting the brush and mowing it down like a chain saw. I was near Cahalane when the ambush started, and we dove behind a fallen tree trunk, which caught ten or fifteen rounds. Then about thirty bullets hit the uprooted dirt mount of the tree. Dirt flew everywhere. Staff Sergeant Perez was behind us and more in the open but wasn't hit. He quickly crawled to us. I thought my heart had stopped. I was so shocked I could hardly breathe. Cahalane blooded his nose on a tree root diving behind the dirt mount, and thought he had been hit at first but realized quickly what he had done. I guess the VC was trying to hit us since he was carrying the radio that day. They liked killing radio men and those around them, and had learned the value that a radio man brought to the fight. He could call for help. Therefore, these Marines became marked targets for gook shooters.

It didn't take long to suppress the Viet Cong attack. They broke it off and disappeared into the bush. I thought to myself at the time, "Man we shot the place up pretty darn good!" I found out why when I took a head count and ammo report just after the fight. Most of my men had their rifles on fully automatic, and expended most of their ammo. Bob chewed on me for quite a while over that mistake. I made sure my men didn't repeat the same thing again. I explained to them, "Use up your ammo, and you do without." That was all I needed to say.

That night, as I sat in my foxhole, I replayed what had happened that day in my mind. My men responded without any leadership from me. They responded on their instincts and training, and I thought about that. I wondered how I would respond if I had to make a decision while under fire. Was I good enough to make the right call? I really labored that night over the entire firefight, most of the time in a cold sweat. I couldn't sleep worrying about it, and there was no one to talk to about it. That would show my uncertainty about my ability. I didn't want anyone dying because of me. I rehearsed my training as squad leader, and I remembered that I was trained to separate myself from the fight, if at all possible, in order to lead. I decided I had participated too much in the actual firefight and not enough accessing the situation. I made myself a promise to not repeat that action. Instead I would respond as I was trained.

Another serious encounter with the enemy took place on Mutter's Ridge on March 20. An Army Twin 40 under the control of Cpl. Mitchell was taken out of operation. Corporal Mitchell was giving support to the action. The tank actually had a "cook off", two rounds exploding at the same time. It happens when too many rounds are fired in succession. The explosion blew two men of the crew out of the turret. One of the exploding rounds hit the ground in front of David Zang and tore his leg up.

Then, to make things worse, the Marines riding a tank accidently dropped C-4 inside the tank causing a fire. Everyone's nerves were fried, so Mitchell and the Marines with him decided to walk back to the base camp. Things like this happened several times, and it couldn't be helped. Staying alive under fire and making the right decision all the time was impossible, and it wore on your nerves. I learned to do what I could and let the rest take care of itself. It caused some heated words to be exchanged, and sometimes a few fist fights, but in the end we stood together. Later that day we would have a Marine wounded on Hill 173 by a booby trap, Danny Higgins.

My squad didn't have much action while at the Rock Pile. We mostly watched the perimeter, and I was thankful for the rest, so to speak. It was hot during the day and foggy in the early morning. Chopper operations were limited due to the weather. Our units lost three Marines to heat exhaustion who were medevac'd out. It was never peaceful and the NVA mortared us every chance they had. I was glad the Marines spent time mentally preparing us for the stress of battle.

Artillery batteries responded with 155-mm Howitzers to the enemy's attacks. They were powerful cannons, and the enemy didn't like the odds. They would break off contact quickly, but the threat of being hit by shrapnel from an incoming mortar or artillery shell remained high. One Marine was wounded by a freak accident when a 60-mm shell exploded short of its target. That wouldn't happen in a thousand years, but it did that day.

Crossing Song Cu River

Our battalion was pulled out of the Razor Back area and sent to Dong Ha, and from there we were air lifted to Da Nang for a three-day rest and recovery time. Cold beer and steak were served. I liked the steak and left the beer drinking to the others. I had Cokes instead. Then we joined the 1st Marine Division for a short operation called Operation Gulf. It was a search and destroy mission in the Song Cu De River area. The mountains boarded the valley on both sides of the river. The canopy was dense and the under-brush very thick. The area had everything to offer including jungle growth, cane fields and ten-foot high elephant grass. The local river dikes were low and crossing them was easy. The Song Cu River was one to eight feet deep depending on the area. It was a perfect scenario for the VC to have an advantage over us, if they chose to fight, but they didn't, and we found ourselves being choppered to an area just south of Da Nang for Operation Canyon.

16

April 1966
An Unknown Marine,
God Rest His Soul

The month of April would include three operations: Operation Canyon, Big Horn and Shawnee. I remember Operation Canyon was conducted in sandy areas with scrub pines about ten feet tall. There were lots of water holes, rice paddies, dry vegetation and dikes. The dikes were especially memorable because of their nature. They were four to five feet tall and two to three feet wide, and they crisscrossed each other in many places. Operation Big Horn was characterized by thunder storms and low hills separated by cultivated areas. I remember the mountains and dense jungle connected to Operation Shawnee. Movement was almost impossible in this region. The temperatures were high and the air very humid, and the trails were narrow and the visibility was limited to only three or four feet into the bush. It was a nerve-racking place to search for the enemy, and once again, I felt they had the advantage.

Things moved quickly that first week of April, and started off with my company being moved to Marble Mountain by truck and then extracted from the Song Cu De region by chopper. CH-46's picked us up and delivered us to Da Nang where the next day was spent supplying ourselves with ammo, C-rations and the necessities for another long stay in the bush. I spent a good part of the day with the other squad leaders in briefing session with our CO, Captain Oots and our XO, 2nd Lt. Bob Brown. I learned we would be joining 1st Battalion 1st Marines and 3rd Battalion 9th Marines in a joint effort. The next day we were going into a well known area of VC activity, and everyone expected a fight with them.

The next morning we loaded onto CH-46's and headed for our objective area. I told my squad we would be going into a hot landing zone (LZ). That morning Brown had notified me that 3rd Battalion 9th Marines had engaged enemy movement and to expect the worst. Our job was to secure the LZ and move north to set up a blocking line to entrap the Viet Cong that were fighting with the other Marine units.

Brown was right about it being a hot LZ. The choppers started receiving fire as soon as they approached the ground. I could hear the bullets piercing the side of our chopper. It sounded like popcorn popping, and they were going right through the paper thin sides of the chopper. The gunner at the door opened up with his M-60 machine gun and the crew chief screamed for us to go. The choppers were hovering about ten feet above the ground. I was the first out the hatch, but the problem was I had a sore ankle from stepping in a hole the week before. I hesitated just long enough to have him shove me out of the chopper. It's a good thing I never saw him again, or one of us would not have gone home. Mitchell ribbed me about being afraid of heights for days.

When I hit the ground, I thought I broke my foot. The pain shot through my leg. My men followed me out of the chopper, and once on the ground we were taking heavy small arms fire from snipers. Their bullets landed too close for our comfort. My men returned the fire and silenced most of the sniper fire for a short time. I managed to move on my foot and get the squad moved to the right flank of the LZ where we dug in. Night came quickly.

That night our corpsman wrapped my foot with some cloth and taped it. It took both of us to get my boot back on. My ankle was black and blue. He said, "We need to get you out of here" to which I replied, "Forget it!" A sore ankle was no reason to be yanked from the field.

The night was terrifying. We received nearly 100 rounds of mortar fire on the perimeter. One round landed near Holdgrafer and me, knocking us over on our backs. He looked at me, and I looked at him with amazement, neither one of us was hit by the blast. Everyone was holding their breath and praying for the night to end. The mortar attacks messed with our minds. We could hear them coming but no one knew exactly where they would hit. It was scary times. Each time the mortars started to fall we held our breath, hoping none fell on us. The mortar attacks were strong enough to make us think they may assault before the night ended. The night crept by.

The next morning we moved out in back of the company as a backup force. The 81-mm mortar unit had fallen about a hundred meters behind us. Somehow the Viet Cong were able to divide them from us, and they were ambushed. Evidently the VC let our platoon walk past the ambush sight before they attacked. Their ambush was quick and effective, and was

140

smart on their part. It took most of the Marines of the 81-mm mortar unit out of action.

The 81's were vital weapons for us. Brown ordered us to move back toward the firefight, and he took the lead. He was a brave Marine and should have been behind us. His skill as a leader was needed more than his guts under fire. Most of the damage had already been done by the time we got to them. Two Marines were dead, one was dying. I saw him in a gully and made my way to him. Brown was using my squad to suppress a sniper's fire. I didn't recognize the Marine. I wish I knew his name. He was in bad shape. I called for the corpsman, HM3 "Doc" Robert Turner. We called him "Doc".

More sniper fire broke out, and we had to take cover. Soon the snipers were silenced and Doc went to work on him. I was holding my hand over a large wound in his side; much of his guts were protruding from his side. The blood was everywhere, and Doc worked feverishly to save him, but it was too late. I will never forget watching the light in his eyes go out. I had never seen a person's eyes glaze over so quickly. His eyes that were full of terror glassed over. It was the most sobering thing I had experienced. His body went limp and suddenly he was much heavier than before. He couldn't even say a word to me and just jerked in pain, moaning.

A lump rose in my throat and I wanted to yell. None of my training had prepared me for this. I wished him back, but death is final. I remember fixing my face like granite and swearing to myself to kill every gook I saw. I laid his head down in his helmet. Doc was stunned, and we said nothing. I am not sure anyone ever realized what happened between us, so much stuff was happening, with people screaming orders and Marines returning fire toward the snipers. We couldn't stay with him. We had to go. Others retrieved his body.

We didn't have time to grieve. We gathered the dead and moved north, trying to catch the rest of our main body. Night overtook us before we caught the main group, but we did join up with the CP. That night one of our patrols captured a VC soldier, and I remember wanting to kill him then and there. I went to where they were holding him and just glared at the bastard, wondering if he was the one who killed the Marine who died earlier this day. He was obviously frightened and rightly so. He sat slumped over, hiding his face. I clutched his jaw and made him look at me. I wanted to see his eyes. There was nothing but terror in his eyes, much like I saw earlier in that fallen Marine. I was forced to leave the area by his guards but none of us valued his life at all.

The next morning we medevac'd the dead and wounded Marines out and continued the sweep northward. The dead were carried to the chopper in ponchos and the wounded on stretchers. It was a grave site. That VC prisoner made a big mistake later in the morning when he broke and ran from his guards, who shot him dead — a fit ending for him. I only wished I had been the one who shot him. Combat changes a person. You think more harshly and bitterness consumes you. That was happening to me.

Later that afternoon we came under mortar fire again, but this time it came from the north and southwest. Fifty or more gooks were spotted. Several of our other squads went after them. A heavy firefight ensued with over sixty rounds being exchanged until the gooks broke the engagement and ran. There were no casualties.

The next day, my squad happened upon three VC soldiers that fired on us from very close range of about twenty meters. A firefight ensued for a few minutes with a fierce exchange of gunfire. We killed all three of them without taking any wounded. So many rounds were fired that we never knew who killed them, but I believe it was Billy Mitchell who opened up on them with his M-60, who silenced them. Later that day at 1420 hours, the VC fired over 100 rounds of mortars at our position.

The mortar rounds were so concentrated that every inch of ground seemed to be exploding. Our only saving grace was their range was off and their rounds hit a few meters shy of their intended target. Still, the devastation of that many rounds withered our morale, and all we could do was hug the ground and try to climb inside our helmets. Horrell, in frustration, returned fire with his M-79, but the VC mortars were out of his range. I knew how he felt. He needed to do something to maintain his sanity. The mortars continued until our 60-mm mortars returned fire. I am not sure if we killed any Viet Cong, but the assault stopped. Rumors were traveling throughout our men that it was the NVA who were harassing us, not the Viet Cong. I am not sure that was accurate information. Two of our Marines were wounded.

Several days passed while we made our way back to the LZ. The Marine units of 1st Battalion 1st Marines and 3rd Battalion 1st Marines met us and began moving back toward the LZ. It was planned for us to sweep a village on the way back but our orders were canceled because our ammo and supplies were dangerously low. Drinking water was at a premium. We were still receiving sniper fire at the LZ, but our company was extracted with no causalities and taken back to Marble Mountain, that to our surprise was not safe. Somehow the VC snipers had penetrated the area at Marble Mountain and we took sniper fire while unloading the choppers.

Later we went from there back to Da Nang, but now I understood why the intense training about boarding and leaving the choppers in the LZ's. Quickness is an essential because you are an open target for the enemy fire. I was thankful for being trained thoroughly. The battle was ever increasing, and as soon as we landed at Da Nang we were loaded onto C-130's and airlifted to Phu Bai. I was dog tired and so were all the Marines in our company. Somehow we needed to muster the fortitude to continue the hot pace our commanders were demanding of us. Our physical conditioning, mental preparation and "esprit de corps" were pushed to the maximum.

Our company would operate out of Phu Bai until April 21. We were told we were joining Operation Big Horn, and our mission would be patrolling the surrounding Phu Bai area. Several of our squads escorted truck convoys carrying ammo to the Marines at Hue. They were able to make the trip in a day, and there was not much action during this time. We didn't have any direct contact with the enemy even though we lost two more Marines to mortar attacks, Pfc. Mickey Miquel and a Corpsman, HM3 Charlie Langenfeld. Charlie was well liked by everyone, and it was a blow to us when he was lost.

Operation Big Horn came to an end on April 21 and Operation Shawnee started immediately. It would utilize the entire battalion. My company was responsible for securing the LZ for the battalion to land. The battalion landed safely and on April 23 we moved into the mountains to conduct a search and destroy mission. We found several old bunkers and fighting holes but no VC. It was raining and continued to rain all night. Everyone was soaked to the bone.

We returned to the LZ to expand it so resupply choppers could land safely. That meant blowing down some trees using C-4 charges. Cutting tree trunks down with C-4 is an easy task. The C-4 is placed around the trunk and detonated. The tree comes down but the branches may still cause a problem for choppers trying to land, and this was the case this time. The choppers still didn't feel safe to land so they dropped our supplies from the tree-top level. Sometimes I wonder what was on the fly boys' minds. If they could land troops, why not supplies? The supplies were dropped from the choppers into the LZ.

We patrolled farther up the mountain on April 26 and set up a patrol base from which we ran patrols until May 6. Again we had no enemy contact, and the worse we dwelt with was the weather and trying to stay dry from the constant rain.

Operation Canyon, earlier in the month, was costly to our battalion, and we lost four Marines over the week's fighting: Cpl. Ed McGrath, Cpl. Art Meadows, Pfc. Allan Gaines, and L/Cpl. Eugene Johnson. We had five wounded. It was the hardest fighting I had been involved in to date, but the worst was yet to come. The month of May would be hell!

17

May 1967
The Battle Of Hickory

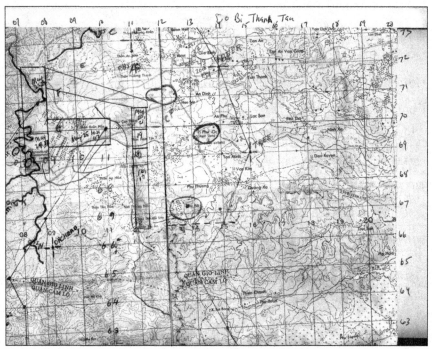

Ayers' Hickory Battle Map

The month of May would bring a conclusion to Operation Shawnee. Operation Hickory would be my last operation. It has become known as the Battle of Hickory and was very costly to our battalion. Our battalion, 2nd Battalion 26th Marines, would fight against a well-trained and disciplined North Vietnamese Army consisting of the 324B NVA and 320th NVA Divisions. The battle was fought in Con Thien, Gio Linh, Cam Lo and Dong Ha, part of what is known as "Leatherneck Square".

Con Thien was located near the DMZ. The Marines had occupied it from December 1966. Together with Marine bases at Gio Linh, Dong Ha and Cam Lo, Con Thien completed the area known to the Marines as "Leatherneck Square." Con Thien was intended to be used as a base for the McNamara Line to prevent NVA infiltration across the DMZ. The firebase was strategically important because it offered unfettered views for fifteen kilometers east to the coast and north into North Vietnam. It was also very vulnerable because it was within range of NVA artillery located north of the DMZ. This artillery was largely immune to counter-battery fire. Con Thien was a location that had to remain in the control of United States forces regardless of the cost to men and equipment. Securing Con Thien would be our objective for the month of May.

Cooling Off – Ayers (with back showing)

During the first week of May our unit moved from the mountain position where we had been running patrols to the valley. There was a stream near where we set up our new base camp. That was nice and we were able to take baths and cool off during the day. Nothing really changed as far as our daily and night routines. We continued our day patrols and night ambushes. Our squads had some success engaging the enemy with one of our night ambushes killing one VC soldier on May 2. Our units lost Pfc. Marion Patrick and L/Cpl. Charles Bricker, who were killed by a booby trap.

On May 8 we moved again by CH-34's to another location, and started a sweep of Prong Dien Soog. The next day we were aided by the 2nd Battalion 9th Marines and 2nd Battalion 4th Marines. Three VC soldiers were killed in fire fights, one was wounded and fifteen captured. The success of the day was not the case with our 2nd Platoon. They met with heavy contact and loss three Marines and had one seriously wounded.

Our platoon was called to help a Recon team who had spotted VC movement. We were choppered to their location but it was a dry run. No VC was engaged by us and that was the norm for the next few days. Our company guarded an artillery battery and our squads kept patrolling the surrounding terrain. We lost one Marine to a booby trap on May 10, Pfc. Earl Watson, from Selma, NC. He was a good man and his death hurt.

May 15 started our battalion's move north to the DMZ. Everyone had an idea that we were going into heavy combat against the NVA regular army. The rumors were being talked about by everyone, and the squad leaders were told to try to keep the scuttlebutt down, but it was no easy task. Marines were writing home and asking for prayers and telling their loved ones things were escalating. The move north was by truck convoy from Phu Bai to Dong Ha, then to Cam Lo.

I wrote Hazel and asked her to pray. Of course, by the time she got the letter the battle was over. I told her we were moving north and by all indications we would meet up with the regular army units of North Vietnam. I wrote things were getting worse and the fighting more dangerous for us. I wrote that we were losing men every day, and I asked her to tell everyone there that I missed them and would see them soon. The letter was short because I didn't have much time to write. I asked her to give my love to Barbara.

The ride to Dong Ha was a mixed event. It was dreary and rainy, but we traveled through the City of Hue. It was a beautiful place. The guys liked it because the pretty Vietnamese girls could be seen walking to their houses and to classes at the local university. Motorbikes and bicycles clutter the streets. The more economically advantaged ones lived in Hue. Their dress and demeanor was totally different than the village people. It would be difficult to believe that later it would be the sight of one of the bloodiest battles of the war when much of that city was destroyed.

I was surprised by our speedy deployment which added more suspense to things. The switch from one truck movement to the next at Dong Ha was quick, possibly because of the heavy artillery fire they had received the night before. I am sure our commanders didn't want us caught in a new attack. It was a mess trying to relocate to the right trucks and keep your gear in order. The stop was slowed somewhat so we could resupply, but in about two hours we headed across the Cam Lo River by way of a pontoon bridge to Route 9. We headed north from Cam Lo.

Cam Lo River pontoon bridge

The conversation was sketchy on the trucks and my men wanted to know what I had picked up while in Dong Ha. Holdgrafer started the conversation off. "Corporal Ayers, rumor has it that the gooks captured some Marines around Con Thien and shot them. What are we headed into?" "Did you hear anything?" Manning piped in, "I bet we are going to see hell up there. I heard that the 9th Marines went against the North Vietnamese Army." Someone in the back of the truck asked, "Is that true?"

They were apprehensive and for good reason. Up until this time, we had fought the Viet Cong with an occasional scrimmage with the regular NVA, and we were always able to overpower them with our weapons and training. I knew the NVA would be a worthy foe. I replied, "What are you Marines worried about? You are the best the Marine Corps have to offer. It is about time we kicked some NVA butts." Powers piped up and snorted, "You didn't answer the question, what are we going to do?" He was right. I remembered what Bones had said, "Be honest and lead. They will follow." I answered, "We have our hands full. The NVA are dug in, well-fortified, heavily armed and well-trained. There is about a battalion of NVA around Con Thien and that is our objective. Find them and destroy them!" There was a strange silence from that moment until we arrived a few miles south of Phu An. Only God knows what they were thinking. Some gazed at the surrounding area and some had their heads bowed, as if to be praying.

1st Squad loading on trucks

We unloaded the trucks at 1930 hours. There was some confusion as we gathered in our areas. Echo Company led off heading northwest. We moved about 4000 meters and set up a bivouac perimeter. Everyone was required to dig a foxhole which was unusual and unsettling for the Marines. Shooting lanes were set up and forward listening posts sent out. Foxtrot Company sent out a patrol to recon the area in front of us, and reported back that there was heavy enemy movement.

Later that night we heard the sound of tanks in the area which caused more apprehension. Sometime later, Ontos units moved into the area. These vehicles were only used when a heavy fight was happening. The tanks were armed with 90-mm cannons, a .50-caliber and .30-caliber machine gun. They could muster a large amount of fire power. They were from the 3rd Tank and Anti-tank Battalions. The Ontos caused more fear in my squad than the tanks. They were anti-tank weapons. I could read the minds of my men. "Do these gooks have tanks?" I had been to a planning meeting and I knew the answer to their concerns. Con Thien had been under heavy attack by two full NVA battalions that had assaulted them on May 8. Their perimeters were breached several times and they were under immense mortar and artillery bombardment from NVA guns across the DMZ. I knew we were in for a good fight. Finally, the opportunity had arrived for us to hurt them! I didn't realize that opportunity would fall on both sides of the fence.

*

The Ringing of the Bells

May 16 started later than planned with Foxtrot moving north at 1100 hours. It was a hot humid day and the temperature would reach 106 degrees. They were finding the going to be tough. The terrain was flat, open fields with thick hedgerows, nearly six feet tall, outlining them. It was almost impossible to maneuver through them. They had to chop their way through these enormous hedgerows.

White Church

Our company was moving up a single lane dirt road boarded by trees and hedges on both sides in the area of Than Bai An. Echo Company was walking point, followed by some of Foxtrot and then my Gulf Company. We passed through a small village. There was a white church with a grey roof just off the road. The villagers were running for cover. Suddenly the church bells began ringing. They were clear and sounded exactly like the ones that rang on Sundays from the churches back home in Salem. They were not muffled but clear sounding. It was an eerie feeling. Goose bumps rose up on my arms. The tanks that joined us the night before were on our flanks. I didn't like it. It was a perfect place for the NVA to ambush us. My squad was on high alert.

The going was slow at first. The heat and our gear were causing problems. Horrell said he was going to pass out but didn't. I could understand it. I was suffering with them. I thought to myself, "How in the world am I going to fight with all this gear I am carrying?" And it was a lot of gear — my helmet, pack, cartridge belt, first aid kit, 200 rounds of M-16 ammo, six C-rations, three canteens of water, an entrenching tool, four grenades, three pop-up flares, a 60-mm mortar round, a 3.5-inch rocket launcher round and a 100 round belt of M-60 machine gun ammo plus my rifle. Each of my men was carrying the same 100 pounds of gear.

The road led us into lush vegetation with pockets of trees separated by dry paddies. We met 1st Battalion 9th Marines and moved through them. They had taken a beating by the NVA. I remember seeing two of my drill instructors from Parris Island lying on an Ontos. Both had been wounded. I spoke to Sgt. Leith and he barked, "Give them hell son!" He was directing the Ontos to the rear with the wounded. I would see him again at the field hospital. Staff Sergeant Strafford wasn't talking, and I never knew how seriously he was wounded. I remember thinking how much I hated these two men when I was in boot camp, and now, I was going to understand why they were so demanding of us. Sergeant Leith was still doing his job. He instilled in me, at that moment, a will to do what it takes to win. Seeing them wounded stiffened my backbone.

Wounded on Ontos

Several minutes later another Ontos passed us with wounded Marines on it. Choppers couldn't land to medevac them so they were being brought to the rear by any means possible. Something caught my eye that stunned

154

me. I saw what looked like Cpl. Black's guitar. It was black and white just like the one he played. It was crushed and thrown on the Ontos along with other gear. I knew in my heart that something awful had happened to him. He would never depart from that guitar. Suddenly the realization that I might soon die embraced me. Fear fell on me like a bolt of lightning, as I turned and watched that Ontos move down the road. It was like a piece of me went with it. I never saw Black from that time on. I can hope he made it home alive.

The order came down for us to move off the road. Mines had been found in the road ahead of us. Echo Company had just crossed a lightly wooded area lined with banana trees and hedgerows. They came upon a 600 meter wide firebreak. It was 1100 hours. They came under heavy attack by the 5th and 6th Battalions of the 812th Regiment of the 324th Division of the North Vietnamese Army of nearly 1200 men. We had found the enemy. The fight was on!

Echo was ordered to pull back to the south side of the firebreak. Foxtrot was ordered to move up on their left flank. A second attempt to take the firebreak failed partly because Foxtrot was ambushed along the road. An air strike was called in to help them but in the meantime they had pulled in their flank guard leaving them open for an ambush. Our XO, Bob Brown was furious. He said that action left us open for an ambush also. Foxtrot's 3rd Platoon was taking a beating, and was pinned down and couldn't move. They were sitting ducks.

Our company was ordered to rescue Foxtrot. We wouldn't get to them until 1300 hours. They would have to defend for themselves for four long hours. The NVA had moved in-between them and us. Foxtrot had taken heavy causalities from every direction. They were surrounded by the enemy, and there were thick hedgerows and open terrain surrounded by trees between us and them.

Jerry Dallape

Jerry Dallape, a member of Foxtrot Company and a recently acquired friend to me, described what they faced in vivid details. He was with the first squad of the 1st Platoon. They were ordered to try to out flank the enemy who had pinned down the 3rd and 2nd Platoons of his company that were taking heavy fire and suffering numerous causalities. It all started with the ringing of the church bells from the church just outside that small hamlet of a few huts, the same as with Echo Company earlier. The hamlet was between the villages of Than Bai An and Nha Tho Bai Son. A NVA sniper opened up on them with an automatic rifle. Then all hell broke loose. Foxtrot was trapped. When the Marines took cover they were in booby trapped terrain. The combination of mortars, artillery, booby traps, machine gun and small arms fire ripped them apart.

Dallape's 1st Platoon moved to the right. They crossed the road approaching the fire fight, moved rapidly through a lightly wooded area lined with banana trees and hedgerows. They found a path leading to the main area of attack by the NVA and where their buddies were pinned down. The three squads of 1st Platoon ran through an opening in the tree line to their front and into an open dry rice paddy. The paddy was outlined by trees on all sides. They were ambushed as they moved across the paddy. The enemy concentrated their fire power on every inch of the paddy, killing or wounding over half of the first squad in seconds. The 2nd and 3rd squads of Foxtrot tried to cross the paddy to help their fallen Marine buddies and met with the same murderous hail of bullets. Their tank support couldn't help them. The NVA attacked them with rocket-propelled grenades. These were deadly against tanks.

The leaders of Foxtrot were wounded, and Cpl. Ron Curley took charge of the platoon. His bravery, in spite of being seriously wounded, earned him the Navy Cross, but his leadership wasn't enough to slow the NVA attack. They went on the offensive and out flanked Foxtrot to their right, splitting the battalion in half. Now Foxtrot was surrounded. Dallape told me he didn't understand how any of them lived through that day. In the middle of the fighting an Ontos attempted to support the men but was quickly taken out by enemy fire. Dallape's machine gun was out of ammo. He had to defer to using his M-16. Bravery was a common valor for those Marines.

Relief was coming. Foxtrot started to receive some heavy fire support. Our artillery had zeroed in on the enemy positions. Huey gun ships were firing into the hedgerows in front of them. Phantom jets pounded Nha Tho Bai. That village was just past where the main fighting was taking place.

It was the main support area for the NVA soldiers. Dallape told me the bombardment took his breath away.

Finally, after four hours, 2ⁿᵈ Lt. Brown led the attack to rescue Foxtrot. We were ordered to fix bayonets. Our third squad, under heavy machine gun fire, advanced on the nearest hedgerow. They took immediate causalities. My squad kept moving down the road. The church bells began to ring again with their menacing sound. We came under sniper fire from the trees along the road. Their shots hit too close for comfort. One bullet struck a tree not two feet from me and the dust from the road was flying from bullets hitting around us. The bark from the impact of the bullet hit my leg. I am not sure how many snipers there were at the start, but we eliminated them quickly.

Marshall shot two snipers at nearly point blank while they were trying to reload, and I shot another one beyond them. Several others dropped from the trees after being hit by our fire. I had wondered what I would do or how I would feel when it came time to know I had killed another person. To be honest, I had so much anger in me that it was easy — maybe too easy. It felt about like shooting ground hogs back home on the farm. I felt no emotion, just satisfaction in hitting the target. Several of the snipers jumped to the ground and ran into the tree line. We found blood where they entered the trees.

We moved through the village that Foxtrot had moved through earlier without taking any major hits, still on the dirt road. Marshall had a graze on his shoulder where a bullet tore through his blouse. Holdgraffer was nicked in the arm, but we didn't have time to think about our wounds. Later a different squad from another unit would take enormous causalities on this same road.

Second Lieutenant Brown called on the radio and ordered us, again, to fix bayonets and to double time up the road and take the area of the banana trees. We stayed close to the edge of the road since we didn't have time to look for anti-personnel mines. We were half on the road and half in the ditch along beside it. Cahalane was so nervous he dropped his bayonet and had to catch up to us. He was not alone. We were all running on pure adrenalin and scared to death.

We ran through the trees to a football-size open dry rice paddy. I stopped us to catch our breath. Bones had come up with his squad on our left, and it sure was good to see Bones even though he was a good ways off. He was like a good omen or something. A quick survey of the situation revealed trees surrounding the rice paddy. These tree lines were only five or six feet deep. There was no other way to the trees but to move through the rice paddy. Our orders were to take the other side, so against my better judgment we started across the paddy.

We were half way across the field when I saw a chopper going down in the distance from being hit by enemy guns. It was smoking badly. Then, all hell broke loose. The NVA opened fire on us from the tree line. We took cover as close to the ground as humanly possible. A worm couldn't get any closer. We could see the flashes from their gun muzzles. We returned the fire as best we could, but the ambush had caught us in a bad spot. Snipers were in trees and had a great advantage over us. If we tried to move we made wide open targets for them. I yelled to Sewell to try to move to the side facing our right and take out the snipers. He did, and his men shot one sniper. Aguon, who was trying to do the same on our left, was not as lucky. The bullets were dancing all around us, and I mean they were hitting within inches of us. Horrell fired several rounds from his M-79 into the trees where the snipers giving Aguon so much trouble were located and silenced the fire from there for a moment. That gave us enough time to pull back to our original position. Bones was having the same kind of firefight.

Staff Sergeant Perez, our platoon sergeant, a scrappy Marine and former boxer, joined me. He said, "We have to get across to those trees." The church bells began to ring again in the distance. I grumbled, "What's with that? I wish someone would stop those bells." We assaulted the tree line a second time with the support of an Ontos. We just about made the tree line under intense small arms fire from the NVA when the Ontos was hit by an NVA rocket. We lost our advantage and had to pull back again. I was amazed no one had been wounded.

The remainder of our company had reached the firefight by this time. We tried to take the area a third time and were repelled by the enemy. They were dug in and very determined to hold that piece of acreage. This time we pulled back to the road and to the cover behind an old rock wall. My heart was racing and my legs felt like rubber. I called for a head count and to my surprise my entire squad was intact, but we were dead tired.

Our company commander, Captain Oots surveyed the battlefield. He ordered Cpl. Bannister to move his M-60 machine gun team to the left side of the fire break. Corporal Mitchell and Jesse Fields were on the right flank with their M-60 machine gun in place. They would give covering fire support for a fourth attempt at taking the objective. We had to take it if we were going to rescue Foxtrot. It seemed the enemy had us and them in their cross-hairs from that position. I was with Bannister along with my squad.

The order came for him and us to open fire on the tree line and hedge-rows to our front. We put down a deadly field of fire, shooting at the flashes coming from the NVA guns. The other squads rose and assaulted the objective. I could hardly believe my eyes as I watched those Marines charge into a deadly hail of bullets. I could see several get hit as I watched through my rifle sights. It was a mixed up mess; screaming orders echoing above the gun fire, Marines yelled like wild men as they charged ahead, shells exploding close enough to take your head off.

Staff Sergeant Perez pulled Mitchell and Fields off their position and sent L/Cpl. Wilton McCarthy to replace them. He needed Mitchell's gun in a position to cover the field from another angle. Fields dumped the spare barrel to their M-60. It was too heavy to maneuver. Perez reported it as lost in battle. Seconds later, a large volume of fire hit the exact place where they had been set up killing McCarthy. His body was later found to be booby trapped. It still hurts Mitchell to think those rounds may have been meant for him and Fields. It's the breaks of combat. No one can figure them out. A sniper bullet hit Mitchell's E-tool on his pack. An inch to either side and it would have hit him in the head. The sound of battle was enormous. The Phantom jets were streaking over our heads and our artillery rounds were rifling past us and hitting what seemed to be beyond the tree line and hedgerow. But this time, the NVA broke off the engagement.

I am not sure where the NVA soldiers went. They just seemed to disappear. They didn't run through the remainder of Foxtrot. We reached Foxtrot and aided in their move to the rear. We hurriedly moved their wounded and dead off of the battlefield, and withdrew to the church with the bells and set up a perimeter. The sight at the church was sickening. There were dead and wounded Marines inside and outside of it. Some were crying in pain and some were smoking a cigarette. It was sobering to me. We were in a real dog fight.

Returning to church – May 16

The church was a busy place. Marines were coming and going with wounded men. It was a tall church building with a small court yard with a well in front of it with good water. The inside must have been a beautiful place before the war arrived. There were overturned statues of Jesus, Mary and a cross. Johnson and I went inside to check it out just before night fell. The wounded were pitiful. Many were crying and some were stiff lipped, some worse than others. The sight of war was horrific. There were dead Marines lying under ponchos off to the side.

Inside church

We sat down for a minute. Johnson asked me, "Phil, do you ever think about God?" "Sometimes," I replied, "How about you?" "Here lately, I've really been thinking about it." I asked, "Thinking about what?" "You know heaven and that kind of stuff. Do you think it really exists?" he questioned. "It must," I replied. "How do you know?" I said, "Because the Chaplain is always reminding us about it. And besides, it says so in our prayer. Remember! We ask God to help us to face 'Thee without shame or fear.' Thee and God are the same, right? And God lives in Heaven, right?" "Yes, you're right." Our talk ended due to approaching darkness. Night had come and I needed to find Cahalane and Frye. We glanced, just for a quick second, at each other to have that re-assurance that everything was alright. Our eyes met. It was one of those moments in two men's lives when a special bond formed. I walked away wondering if there was a Heaven and a God. I hoped so but in the midst of all I was seeing, I wondered. My deal with God didn't seem to be working very well.

The NVA harassed us all night with incoming mortar fire, and they made a few attempts to breach our perimeter. Cahalane, Frye and I set up a listening post about seventy-five meters in front of our perimeter. We were listening for movement. It was a sleepless night. One of us was supposed to sleep while the other two remained awake, but that didn't work on this night. We could hear the gooks talking in the distance and we heard the clanking of metal, like mortar tubes hitting together. We guessed they were moving to a different location during the night. I radioed it back to the CP but they said to maintain our position and not to engage them. Cahalane asked me if I thought we would make it out of this fight alive. Rumor had it that we were surrounded by a full division of the North Vietnamese Army. He loved his girl and missed her. I told him, "Without a doubt." That still haunts me even today.

During the rest of the night my mind was captured by the question Johnson had asked me about Heaven. I thought back to Mrs. Lamourant and her prayers. Her faith was real. She believed in a God that could deliver people from trouble. Hazel told me about Jesus who loved me and my need to accept Him as my Savior. The more I thought, the more frustrated I became. I remembered my experience on my rock back home and the peace I felt. But now it all seemed meaningless to me except to offer comfort to my men. I mumbled to myself, "Then why are we here, God, and why are we dying?" Cahalane heard me say something and asked what I said. I told him to stay focused on the bush. "I'm just talking to myself!"

I look back on that day, and realize it was not without heavy losses and unheralded bravery on the part of our Marines that we took the day. The accounts of bravery are too numerous to tell them all. A few stand out. Corporal Wright led his fire team of four Marines against a hedgerow blazing with automatic gun fire. His team killed the NVA soldiers in the gun position inside the hedgerow. He received the Silver Star for his courage.

Corporal Jim Hart, Jr., one of our radio operators, took things into his own hands and attacked a bunker. He was hit by a mortar in his leg, but kept advancing on the bunker. A sniper shot him in the head and he still reached the bunker and killed the NVA soldiers in it. He received the Silver Star.

When the order was given to attack, Cpl. Richard Moffitt's squad, on our right flank, was pinned down immediately. He singled-handedly assaulted a machine gun bunker. He took it out and silenced the enemies' left flank support. He received the Navy Cross for his heroism. He was asked later, "What was going through your mind when you attacked that gun?" He replied, "Nothing."

Second Lieutenant Bob Brown was another hero of the day. He led five men from the command group in an attack on the NVA to remove several wounded Marines. He was shot in the neck but refused medevac. He received the Bronze Star.

We had fought toe-to-toe with North Vietnamese's best for more than four hours, sometimes close enough to use bayonets on them. They were well-entrenched in half-moon bunkers with the help of thick hedgerows. They had well placed spider holes in front of them that surprised us and showed they were well-trained and had good tactics. They had good weapons such as AK-47'rifles, 12.7-mm machine guns, stick-handed potato masher grenades, mortars and artillery. They were seasoned troops, dressed in green cotton uniforms with green boots, and they were willing to fight.

They had set up a "U- shaped" ambush with gun positions on each side of the fire break. They were patient and waited for us to move into the middle of the "U- shaped" ambush before engaging us. They had two lines of defense behind that original point of contact. These lines of bunkers were fifty meters behind each other. They fought with eight of their soldiers in each bunker, and I admit we had never faced this kind of foe to date.

The cost of that day was high. We were dangerously low on ammo and had very little water. It would take the next day to get more ammo. Dong Ha medical hospital was overwhelmed with our wounded and there was not enough room for our dead Marines. It was a sickened, gut-wrenching feeling to see all the dead Marines lying under ponchos along the dirt road we had just captured from the NVA soldiers. Billy Mitchell said he saw brave Marines sobbing as they gathered their dead comrades.

We were told fifteen Marines were killed on this day and sixty wounded. We had killed seventy-nine NVA soldiers. The smell of death was in the air and is never forgotten. The wounded had to be moved on tracked vehicles, which slowed their treatment. Choppers couldn't land because it was too hostile.

We thought about our loses, especially how L/Cpl. Wilton McCarthy was killed, and his body being booby trapped by the gooks, and how it took a special effort to recover it. Our platoon leader wanted to detonate the booby while McCarthy's body was still on it. I remember that made us as mad as hell. We removed the booby trap before moving his body. Corporal Dicky Krumn was killed. He was a wrestler from Blue Earth High School and a neat Marine. Corporal Wright, Cpl. Collet and L/Cpl. Shurtz were wounded. Many others were wounded but didn't report it.

*

Much Bravery Shown Today

May 17 started at 0800 hours. We moved out from the perimeter and the church area to rejoin Foxtrot and Hotel Companies. Our platoon was re-supplied around noon with ammo, C-rations and one canteen of water. Water was like gold to us. The orders came down that we were going to use a frontal assault tactic on the firebreak that had given us so much trouble the day before. Everyone was terrified of that idea but our commanders knew the whole picture, and we didn't. I remember wondering if the soldiers in Pickett's charge felt this way.

It took some time for the companies to move into striking positions. Our company was on the left flank and Echo Company would take the right flank. Foxtrot, which had lost most of its men in the fight yesterday, was assigned the road. Hotel Company would advance behind Foxtrot. Two tanks accompanied our company and Echo Company had five tanks with it. Our 2nd Platoon would lead the assault with the help of our tanks. I really didn't understand why we had to do this over again, when the day before we had captured the terrain. I wondered, "Why did we give it back?" But here we were, and it was time to move. The truth is that we were there and no one else, so the job was ours to complete.

The assault made it half way across the firebreak when the NVA artillery and mortars opened up on us. One tank with the 2nd Platoon was knocked out of the fight immediately when it hit a land mine. However, the tanks proved to be too much for the NVA soldiers to with-stand. They ceased their contact with us and retreated. We reached the tree line and the hedgerow just behind it with few wounded. The tanks were using shotgun shells against them, and they were deadly. Their one shot equaled about a hundred Marines firing rifles at the same time. I was thankful, at first, because we reached the tree line quickly. I thought, "Maybe today will be easier. Maybe they got their fill of us yesterday!"

It quickly became apparent that the NVA had maneuvered us into a trap for the second straight day. Once again they had managed to catch us in their U-shaped ambush. Our leaders had made a mistake by over expanding our frontal assault line. We were far too spread out. Our 2nd Platoon was hit hard, so 2nd Lt. Brown led us up to their left to help relieve the pressure on them and to hold their position. The enemy fire was vicious. We could hear the bullets whistling past our heads. It seemed the intensity of the enemy concentration of fire increased on our flank as soon as we moved up.

My squad was pinned down immediately by machine gun fire and the other Marines were facing heavy incoming artillery. The NVA had led us directly into their field of fire. It was all planned by them, and to make things worse, they used tear gas shells. I recognized we were not going to do well trying to stay where we were pinned down, so I shouted for the men to move forward. I yelled, "We have to get out of the mortar range!" "Let's move!" Brown was demanding the same move from his location. My men were outstanding. They advanced about a hundred meters, shooting as they went, before encountering heavier machine gun fire. Once again, we were pinned down, but this time we found some cover behind some fallen trees. But we had outrun their mortars.

Assaulting tree line – May 17

These few minutes seemed like an eternity. Combat is strange like that. Sometimes, the time creeps by and it's like you are suspended in time, in slow motion. The enemy was entrenched in bunkers. Our platoon and my squad had moved to within thirty meters of the NVA positions. The fighting was savage. The tanks were being hit by enemy RPG rounds and we lost another tank. My second fire team, Sewell, Frye, Manning and Cahalane, reached one bunker and was fighting the NVA soldiers in a hand-to-hand confrontation. They killed them but things kept getting worse.

The NVA soldiers had let us move past many of them who were now popping up out of spider holes behind us. We were being shot at from every direction. One raised up no more than two feet from me. My close-ness to him surprised him enough that he hesitated, and I shot first. He dropped dead back down into the pit. To make sure no more gooks were with him I dropped a grenade down the hole.

My squad was taking care of themselves by this time. Nothing I could have said would have helped our cause. We were all busy saving each other. All my former worries were useless. The firefight was deafening.

The NVA soldiers threw several grenades at us. Luckily, none of them exploded. Maybe prayer was working. They paid with their lives. My squad and our platoon silenced the enemy at that hedgerow and came out on the other side. We were surprised to see another open field. The rest of the companies were keeping pace.

Second Lieutenant Brown ordered us across the field. Our 3rd squad had moved up on my squad's right flank. He obviously didn't want us to lose the momentum we had gained. But what he didn't realize was that the NVA had fallen back to their second defense line. It was another entrenched bunker complex. We were barely into the field attempting to take the right side of that entrenched bunker complex when the enemy opened up on us again, but this time they used a .51 caliber machine gun.

The bullets from a .51 caliber machine gun were twice the size of normal bullets and could cut a man in half when one bullet hit him. My heart was in my throat and I could hardly breathe. My legs were burning like fire and the sweat was pouring off of me. The same was true for all of the men, and to make things worse, the gooks had pulled their mortars back and now we were in range of their mortars again. It seemed every inch of ground was being hit by bullets or shrapnel. The incoming bullets were so concentrated that they literally cut the tops out of a stand of banana trees to our right. Corporal Mitchell couldn't believe his eyes. He said, "It looked a giant knife leveled them with one swoop." I will never understand how we survived that fight unless someone was praying back home at that very moment.

I looked to my right and saw several Marines, from Echo company, go down. Our platoon and their company had moved to the same ground. They fell in exposed positions and were sure to be killed in seconds. My squad was not moving at that moment. We couldn't. Something inside of me moved me into the open and toward those fallen Marines; something many fellow Marines were doing to help their buddies. They were about fifty meters away. Just as I reached the first one, a bullet hit the heel of my left boot. The impact spun me around and knocked me to the ground. I crawled to the first Marine and pulled him into an artillery shell crater in the ground and headed for the other one. He was a few meters away and wrenching in pain. I reached for and pulled at his flak jacket. He was caught on something under him and didn't move. I lost my balance and fell backward. The force on my hand dislocated my left thumb. I looked at my hand and sat down on my butt all at the same time. My thumb was twisted and facing inward. It hurt like hell but I couldn't help that at the moment.

I was sitting upright in the middle of enemy fire. I jerked his arm and pulled violently on his flak jacket. He moved. I dragged him to the same place as the first Marine. I looked back toward my squad and realized S/Sgt. Perez was screaming his head off for me to get back to my squad. It seemed an enemy gunner had taken aim at me because bullets were hitting everywhere around me. I felt the heat off one as it ripped through my blouse. I didn't wear a flak jacket. The one Marine was bleeding badly. I grabbed him by his vest and dragged him back to Doc who had moved to the crater. How he made it there I don't know. Not enough could be said about the bravery of the Navy corpsmen in battle. They were exceptional!

I bolted for my squad and made it to them. My foot was burning with pain. Perez was in my face, "Don't ever do that again. They can defend themselves. Your place is here with your own men. You understand me, Marine?" "Sure!" I barked back. My mind flashed back to that day in the swimming pool at Parris Island and my failure to measure up. I was feeling that pressure. Stress was setting in and in another minute we probably would have fought each other. A few mortar rounds falling close to us changed our thoughts.

My thumb was throbbing and my foot was still burning. It so happened to be the same one I hurt jumping out of the chopper some time back. Johnson saw me holding my hand and crawled to me. He insisted on me showing him my thumb. Before I knew it he pulled it back into the right direction. I about died but it helped. It looked like the bone was about to stick out of the skin. Later the Doc splinted it for me. I had to simply endure the pain in my ankle.

It is times like these when the true grit surfaces in some men. Brown recognizing the situation at hand, urged us forward. To our right flank, S/ Sgt. Perez had taken up a position with the 2nd squad that was engaged in a point-blank firefight. Perez, himself took out the machine gun nest. Bones broke cover and rushed a machine gun bunker throwing a white phosphorus grenade into it, killing the enemy gunners. Corporal Cauble was able to move close enough to throw a grenade into another bunker and then empty a full magazine of rounds into the enemy position, killing the NVA soldiers there.

While they were busy fighting for their lives, two of Bones' men, L/ Cpl. Warren Nooman and Pfc. "Bulldog" Brunton, were caught in the open. They were wounded numerous times but kept returning the fire. Their bravery kept the enemy focus off of Bones. The fighting was close and in several cases hand-to-hand again. My mind was racing and my thoughts were wild . . . kill anything that moves. A thought flashed across my mind that one of the D.I.'s in boot camp had said during bayonet training. "Never leave your feet when hand fighting the enemy. When you do, you are dead!"

It's strange what goes through your mind when your life is dependent on killing or be killed. It all happens in seconds of time. Bones received the Silver Star. Brunton and Noonan received the Bronze Star.

Just as we were about to gain an advantage, the NVA soldiers sprang an attack against our rear. They had come up out of spider holes again. They were so well trained that we didn't see these positions as we advanced. They were camouflaged to appear like all the rest of the ground. I am not sure we could have found them anyway, while fighting forward. There was no time to probe for sniper holes.

Again, we were pinned down and being pounded by enemy fire from two directions. Our company commander, Captain Oots, ordered the assault to withdraw. We fought our way back through the enemy to our first position. He ordered the tanks forward in spite of their losses to demolish the bunker complex. They did a great job in spite of being under heavy rocket attack from the NVA. The tanks were able to overpower them again for us. The NVA soldiers broke off the engagement and withdrew again. I asked for a head count and ammo status. We were all still together but very low on ammo and grenades. I saw some of the men guzzling their water. I scolded them. Water was in short supply, only one canteen per man, and I wasn't sure when we would be re-supplied. I think everyone was questioning, "What the hell just happened?"

Word came to us that our battalion command post had been mortared during our assault. I wondered how the NVA could move so freely as to get to a position where they could mortar our people from the rear of us. Their battle plan was effective, and they were causing us to question our objective. They fired over forty 82-mm mortar rounds into the headquarters. Our battalion commander, Lt. Col. Figard, was wounded in the attack

173

and the battalion radioman lost a leg. I later learned this was the reason we were ordered to withdraw from our assault. They were mortared again two hours later, wounding six more Marines. All together two hundred rounds fell on them. It was hard to imagine how any of them survived.

Once again we found ourselves digging in for another long night of uncertainty. We had paid a heavy price that day for the small amount of ground we had captured. Both Marines and NVA soldiers had died this day and our ability to gather the dead and wounded was hampered by the constant mortar rounds falling on our position and snipers shooting at anything that moved within the perimeter. This went on all night. Once again our supplies had to be dropped into our perimeter by choppers from tree-top height.

The enemy mortars prevented them from landing. We expected this would happen but the most damaging thing was that we couldn't get fresh water. The water bottles exploded upon impact with the ground. We were forced to search our dead comrades for their canteens and ammo. I felt sick at having to remove another Marine's property. Moving the dead weight of a human body is not easy, and it is complicated when it is someone you know who just hours before was able to talk and laugh and move on their own. Cauble said it best: "Decades would not dull the horror!" I know the others felt the same, but we were in desperate need of water and ammo. I know Manning threw up after trying to drink from a dead gook's canteen. They drank some kind of syrupy tea. I took a flak jacket off one of the dead Marines. Somehow I felt I had left his lifeless body naked, but I figured he wouldn't mind. Things were bad!

That night we put listening posts outside the perimeter. Just like the night before the outpost reported hearing the NVA moving around. Several of them made the mistake of coming too close to one of the outposts and were shot dead by a Marine with a shotgun. I am not sure where the shotgun came from or who carried it. Four more were killed later that night, as they approached one of our positions. My squad didn't send anyone out this night. I was glad because my hand was hurting like everything. We guarded from our fox-holes, but we had orders to fire on any movement outside of our position. I'm not sure why we were given permission to do that because it was not customary practice. I figured the commanders expected a night attack, and in fact, they did try to slip inside several times but with no success. None of us got any sleep. Occasionally, you could smell their sickening smoke in the breeze from whatever they smoked. They were that close.

The mortars, including CN and CS gas rounds, kept coming all through the night. Many Marines were unofficially wounded during the night. Very few corpsmen were left to keep count of the wounded and regular riflemen were being asked to serve as medics. The good news was that reinforcements were coming; 2nd Battalion 9th Marines would join our right flank and 3rd Battalion 9th Marines would move up to help our left flank.

Probably the most sickening thing of this entire day was the stench of NVA dead bodies. They were lying all over our parameter. Wherever they were killed is where they remained, and many of us were becoming sick on our stomachs at the smell of dead flesh and garlic. The gooks loved their garlic. They were kind of stupid in a way because that particular garlic smell gave their positions away on many occasions. We had to do something or all of us wouldn't be able to fight, so we started to bury the dead NVA soldiers in very shallow graves. Sniper fire hindered our efforts. Burying the bodies helped, but it didn't totally solve the problem. I will never forget that smell as long as I live.

May 17 was a sad day. We lost three Marines and had one hundred wounded. Corporal Johnston, Pfc. Jerome Parris, and Pfc. Charles Eakins had died. These were courageous men. Corporal Bradley recalls Eakins' bravery. He exposed himself to enemy fire going to get M-60 ammo for his team leader and gunner. He brought back 300 rounds. He was killed while fighting beside Bradley later that day. He was nineteen-years old, my age, and from Clay, Kentucky. The Platoon Diary read simply, "Much bravery shown today!"

Tank assault – May 17

The one bright thing about the day was mail call. The choppers had dropped a large sack of mail. It wasn't easy getting it separated and passed out to the men but we managed. Several of my men, including me, received letters from back home. I was happy for them. It would be difficult to read them without light but we found a way. My letter was from Hazel. She seemed concerned for me. I hadn't written to her in some time. I'm sure she had not received my last letter since she didn't mention it. She told me how things were in Salem. She hadn't seen Mike. She was glad the days were getting warmer. Her letter was mostly small talk but appreciated by me. Barbara was doing fine and studying for finals. Hazel said she was stressed over one of her classes. There was no mention of an upcoming prom dance. I couldn't help but wonder if she was going. I thought to myself, "I hated school and exams, but I sure wouldn't mind changing places with someone now."

Pfc. Cahalane

Cahalane received a letter from his girlfriend. I could see his entire demeanor change. He had been down for some time, but not this evening. His spirits were high. I am not sure what she said to him in those letters but they sure worked in his favor. She sent him a new picture of herself. He stared a hole through it the rest of the night. He put it in his pocket next to his heart the next morning. The ones who didn't have mail didn't seem to be bothered. They were tired and simply glad to be alive!

*

Valor Distinguished the Day

May 18 started at 0800 hours. We moved north accompanied by tank and Ontos support at 1100 hours. Our objective was to push the NVA into the 3rd Battalion 4th Marines who had choppered into the DMZ near the Ben Hai River. They would act as a blocking force to stop the retreating North Vietnamese Army. That morning we were re-supplied with ammo, water for our one canteen, and received gas masks from Dong Ha. Many of us had more than one canteen but we were only allowed water in one of them. Water was a premium, especially when the temperature would rise to 100 degrees. We moved our wounded to the rear. We lost two Marines and had five wounded by incoming mortar fire during the morning. There seemed to never be a time of rest for us. We were constantly being harassed by the enemy.

Our movement northward started at 1110 hours with Echo Company and our Gulf Company leading the advance, followed by Foxtrot and then Hotel. My squad had moved to the right flank of our platoon and about two hundred meters when we came under heavy machine gun and mortar fire. Two NVA battalions had slipped within a short distance of our perimeter during the night and took up positions in their former bunker positions. This time it seemed they had learned how to adjust their mortar fire for close-range shelling. I shouted for my men to double time across the opening and into the tree line to our front. The NVA soldiers who were in the tree line opened up on us with overwhelming gun fire. They outnumbered us.

We were pinned down in the middle of the field. It seemed that was becoming a common thing lately. This time it was worse than any of the previous days. I got on the radio and literally had to scream into the mouth-piece in order to be heard. The noise of battle was that loud. "We are being hit hard . . . . Heavy causalities being taken. . . Can I pull back?" "No!" came the answer. "Push forward!" My mind was racing in desperation. "Don't panic Philip!" The entire platoon was advancing on the left side of us. Just as I put the receiver down, thirty mortar rounds hit in middle of us. They were shelling us with thirty rounds at a time and then they would re-locate their position to avoid our artillery's response. The luck of my squad had run out, and we took numerous hits. My men seemed paralyzed in place.

Marshall, Sewell, Moore, Horrell and Cahalane were hit immediately. Frye and Cox had minor shrapnel wounds. I saw the round hit at the feet of Cahalane. The round exploded between his legs with such force that it threw dirt on us. He didn't cry out or say much of anything at first. He had both legs badly mangled and nearly severed. I called for a corpsman. Private First Class Powers crawled to him. I screamed, "Stop the bleeding! Use his boot strings!" My blood was running hot, and I was trembling with anger toward the enemy. I, also, felt like my chin had been hit with a hammer. Then I saw my blood dripping on the ground. Fright gripped me at first. Seeing your own blood shakes you. I felt my chin and realized I had a long cut under it. I could feel my chin bone. The wound had cut deep into my chin bone. I realized I had been hit in my lower back and right arm. Both were bleeding.

Pinned down in crater – May 18

I knew we had to move. Just to our front were three deep shell craters. I motioned for Johnson, Holdgraffer, and Aguon to move up to the craters. They began crawling fast and very low to the ground toward them. Thirty more mortar shells hit very near to the craters. Flying dirt covered them, but they kept moving forward and made it to the craters. There was no way Marshall, Sewell, Moore, Horrell and Cahalane would be able to move fast enough to make it there. They were about fifteen meters behind me. I crawled on my hands and knees to where Marshall and Sewell were lying and encouraged them to try to move to Johnson's position. Together we made it to him. I returned to help Horrell. He was able to put weight on his legs but we had to move in a low and crouched posture. He couldn't crawl. It is a miracle we were not shot. The bullets were hitting in front and to the side of us. I remember spitting dirt out of my mouth from the ground being churned up in front of me. We made it to the crater.

Johnson and Holdgraffer were returning fire into the tree line. I told them to keep shooting and was turning to go after Powers and Cahalane, but Powers had already made the ditch beside us. Somehow he managed to get Cahalane there too. Cahalane was nearing unconsciousness. I was fighting back the tears. I couldn't believe his legs were so messed up. Then it hit me. They were gone.

L-R, Billy Mitchell and Fields

Frye and Cox had shrapnel wounds but they made it to the ditch. Frye was carrying the radio. I crawled to him and answered a call from S/Sgt. Perez. His voice was troubled. "Can you take the tree line?" I am not sure why I answered the way I did. "Yes!" Pure adrenalin had taken over. Johnson, Holdgraffer, Frye, Cox, Aguon and I rushed the tree line in a frontal assault. We were spread out in a parallel line about ten meters apart. I didn't realize that somehow Cpl. Mitchell and his ammo man, Jesse Fields, had advanced to the hedgerow on our right side. They were out ahead of us and engaged in a firefight with an NVA machine gun bunker. The beautiful thing was that they took some of the fire that had been directed at us. They knocked out the enemy guns. We all made it to the trees. The fighting there was hand-to-hand. It lasted only minutes. More NVA soldiers shot at us from another position and, I think, actually hit some of their buddies in their backs.

I received the Navy Commendation Metal with Combat "V" for the day's action. Actually my men should have been awarded it! The date on my citation says for action done on May 17, but I think the date should have been May 18. There was so much confusion at the time.

Just on the other side of that tree line was another hedgerow, and it was full of NVA soldiers. We spotted the gun positions in the hedgerow and immediately opened fire on them. We didn't know it at the time but the 3rd squad to our left was still pinned down and Bones' squad to their left was in heavy combat also. Bones had managed to move his squad to the hedgerow. I learned later that Bones was wounded and evacuated to the rear. My squad managed to get within striking distance of the hedgerow. The enemy wasn't focused so much on us. Our entire platoon was engaged. It had become a major free-for-all.

My squad started to be peppered with small arms fire. I hit the ground along with the other men. Fear turned my blood cold. I landed just inches from an anti-personnel mine. I saw the three prongs sticking up out of the ground. The first thing I thought of was what if I landed on one? If I was lying on it, which meant my body weight was keeping it from exploding. My blood curled. I searched the ground around me and couldn't see any others, and none of my men on either side of me seemed overly concerned with any mines. The bullets were getting closer all the time. I had to move.

I sprang to my feet and ran a few meters and dived into any enemy bunker. My men were rushing forward. I landed on top of a dead NVA soldier. It was like I had landed on a snake. I rolled to the side just in time to realize there was a live gook under him. I guess he was playing possum. I had my bayonet on my rifle. I stuck him in his throat and shot him at the same time. Blood flew all over me. I thought my heart would jump out of my chest. I climbed out of the bunker and clawed my way through the hedgerow to the other side. My squad had passed through it and had started to dig in. They were digging temporary holes to get some defense from the incoming bullets. The holes were no more than ten inches deep but they provided enough cover to not be totally exposed to enemy bullets.

I came out of the thicket near Johnson, who was on the ground. He rolled onto his back and saw me. I think he thought I was a gook at first and was going to shoot. His facial expression looked like he had seen a ghost. "Damn!" he exclaimed. "What happened to you?" I was covered with the gook's blood. Later that night we talked and I told him what had happened. Johnson was probably my best friend at the time and I could trust him. I wiped the blood off my blouse with dirt, or at least, I changed the color of it. We kept returning the enemy fire.

I heard the sound of gun-fire in front of and to our left. We had stopped being shot at for the moment. I figured we had fallen behind so I ordered the men to move ahead. We moved across a small opening between hedge-rows, and stopped just long enough to catch our wind. We approached a stand of bamboo trees and moved through them. We took up positions in some shell craters just on the other side. The order came to stand our ground in place.

Corporal Mitchell had taken a position under the remains of a tree. Just in front of him was a dead NVA soldier in a trench, about twenty feet in front of them. That was always a horrifying sight. The thing is, there seemed to be an NVA soldier standing up a few hundred feet farther ahead of them. Fields grabbed an M-16 rifle and shot at the figure. Perez came running to see why they were still firing. Well, the NVA soldier turned out to be a scarecrow dressed in an NVA uniform. There's nothing like a little laughter in the midst of a very serious day of fighting. It relieved some of the tension in Mitchell's mind. He had been shot three times that day; one round went through his poncho on his pack, one of his six canteens had a hole torn in it by shrapnel and his blouse pocket was sliced by mortar fragments. So killing a scarecrow seemed fitting to ease the stress!

I couldn't believe what I heard next. It sounded like jet fighters coming toward us and it was. They came in at dangerously low levels and dropped napalm and bombs into the enemy positions not more than fifty meters in front of us. The sound and heat from the explosions jarred our teeth and caused us to bury our heads in the ground. The earth from the bombs exploding landed on us. Man, they were close. During the air strikes, 2nd Battalion 9th Marines had finally moved closer to our position on our far right flank. The problem was, of course, we didn't know it. Those air strikes gave us the needed break in the fighting that allowed us to regroup.

My men were exhausted and dying for water. We had heard tales of other Marines who were so thirsty that they cut holes in the bamboo and sucked out the liquid. Bamboo trees were everywhere around us. They said it tasted like turpentine. None of us was about to test their story. It was about 1600 hours. And besides, Manning had already tried it.

Catching rain water in ponchos

We needed water in the worse way. I couldn't belief it. Relief came from heaven. It clouded over and rained in a matter of minutes. The first shower didn't last long enough for us to take advantage of it, but a second afforded us the opportunity to catch the rain water in our ponchos. It rained hard for about ten minutes and we were able to fill our canteens. Was it a gift from God? Was this the answer to someone's prayer? I couldn't help but wonder.

The rain left just as quickly as it had come. Most of us were still bleeding from our wounds. The rain gave us a chance to wash the blood off our clothes and wounds. We depended on each other to patch us up. One of our last corpsman, "Doc" Bob Turner from Portland, Maine, had been killed trying to reach a wounded Marine. The news of his death was devastating. He had been with us from the very beginning of my tour. I just sat there in disbelief. The loss was almost unbearable.

My arm had stopped bleeding but my back and chin wouldn't stop. I found it hard to hold a compress on my chin and do what I needed to do. Johnson pulled the wound on my back together and taped it closed. I have no idea where he found the tape. He did the same for my chin. I asked him how bad it looked. He said, "You'll live." The determination to live was so obvious on their faces.

The order came down to us from Lt. Col. Masterpool to continue the attack. Our company commander, Captain Oots, took the initiative. I didn't see him but everyone said he walked right to the front of the line in the midst of enemy fire. It inspired our Marines to follow him. Bravery was being shown everywhere and by all ranks on the battlefield. It was around 1630 hours.

This time the assault had our battalion on the left flank and 2nd Battalion 9th Marines on the right. The remaining tanks took the lead in front of us. Almost immediately we were showered with mortars and artillery. There was a stand of banana trees directly in front of us, and behind them another hedgerow. Every one of us knew the gooks would be there. Our only saving thought was that the napalm the fighter jets had dropped had done its job. Our thoughts were right, and we received very little resistance at this hedgerow. We did find many NVA bodies fried by the napalm. The smell of burning flesh permeated the air. Even those of us who had seen death up close had a problem with the smoldering bodies. The napalm was still burning the flesh on many of them with smoke still rising from their bodies.

Dead NVA soldier

My squad broke through the hedgerow along with the rest of our platoon to our right. I couldn't believe my eyes. There was more dense foliage in front of us. It was about one hundred fifty meters away. Another field lay directly to our front. It appeared to have been a cultivated area at one time. The NVA soldiers had decided to make their stand there. Our tanks once again took the lead. But even with their fire power, the enemy had us out gunned. Their anti-tank weapons and the intense mortar barrage were too much for us to advance, plus, they opened up on us with small arms and machine gun fire again. Almost immediately we lost a tank due to a direct hit from an enemy RPG rocket.

Pfc. Lancaster being treated - May 18

The NVA fire power was too much for us to withstand and we were stopped after advancing only one hundred meters. The mortars started to hit their marks again. Things were really bad again for us. In fact, we probably would have all died at that point had not several other tanks arrived on the scene. Those tanks were awesome to see. They were firing their rounds at point blank range and they were finding their targets. The explosions from the tank rounds killed two or three gooks at a time. Their bunkers were torn apart by the explosions. The enemy finally broke off the fight. Our battalion seized the area and set up defensive positions for the night. Later that evening, 2nd Battalion 9th Marines sent their Foxtrot Company to reinforce us.

That night the mortars continued to fall on us, and this time the mortars came from our right and left flank. It seemed the NVA had moved into positions on our flanks, but that was impossible because we thought we had covered our flanks. The enemy tried twice to breach our perimeter but was beaten back both times. One of those attacks was in front of us. We cut them to pieces with intense automatic fire and hand grenades. Mitchell fired over 100 rounds that night with his gun team. Two of the gooks fell just inches from our foxholes. The night was another very long and tense one.

The dead gook bodies lying in front of us were a constant reminder of what might happen next. No one knew if they would counter-attack us. They hadn't tried an all-out night assault, so we figured that would be their next move but it didn't come. Actually, they were withdrawing their main force and the action that night was just a diversionary tactic by them.

Moving through elephant grass

I moved along our line and re-assured my men. They were scared and so was I. We had been fighting at close range for three days. We had lost our comrades and friends. We were wounded and should be sent to the rear but we knew that would not happen. Our battalion needed us to stay and fight, and I don't think anyone really wanted to leave the fight anyway. It had become very personal. Some of their talk of wanting to go to the rear was just their way of letting off steam. I know they were hurting though, because I was. My ankle was swollen to the point that I was afraid to take my boot off. My arm was hurting from the shrapnel wound and my chin never had stopped aching. I didn't really feel my back wound and the good news was that nothing was bleeding now.

Our battalion had taken heavy losses this day. We had three Marines killed and 104 wounded. We were not alone in our losses. The 2nd Battalion 9th Marines had suffered heavy losses also. The 3rd battalion 9th Marines on our battalion's left had made no contact with the enemy on this day. They were the fortunate ones.

*

The Cost of Winning

During the night the NVA retreated to the northeast and northwest leaving behind enough soldiers to hinder our movement. May 19 would be a frustrating day compared to the previous days. It was a day when we were hurt by the enemy but we had no opportunity to fight back. We were moving into hill country, and there were fewer hedgerows which everyone was tired of seeing. The tallest hill was 190 meters in altitude. There was vegetation ranging from brush to small strands of trees. The trees, for the most part, were spread out. This allowed for easy movement. Some of the valleys had open spaces and several areas had elephant grass ranging from six feet to fifteen feet in height and the valleys were separated by burned out forest.

Our day started at 0500 hours when we received our ammo rations and C-rations. Our water situation was better. Most of us had taken extra canteens from our fallen comrades. I carried six with me, which I had filled with the rain water yesterday. The NVA artillery shelled us at 0800 hours wounding ten Marines. They hit us again at 0850 hours with fifteen rounds of 82-mm mortars, and another eighteen Marines were wounded. The NVA had a new battle plan, and it became obvious very quickly. They would harass and frustrate us until we made a mistake by avoiding any direct confrontation.

It was during the second mortar attack that we lost 2nd Lt. Bob Brown. That was a real blow to our company. He was a great leader and a good Marine. Several times he had shown extreme bravery under fire and saved the day on May 17. He had become a good friend to me. He was struck in his arm by shrapnel.

L-R, Leroy, Marinez, Capt. Oots

Catherine Leroy, a twenty-two year old reporter from France, was also wounded during that attack. She was a beautiful woman and person. I remember she always wore her brown hair in pigtails. She was a tiny woman, only five feet tall and eighty-five pounds, but she had a heart of steel. She was determined to tell our story and faced the same enemy fire as we did. She carried three different cameras: a Nikon, a Nikormat and a

Leica. They were destroyed by the shrapnel and saved her life on this day. She had thirty-five shrapnel wounds and a broken jaw.

She would undergo a three-hour operation to repair the damage to her legs, neck, arms, chest, back and face. It didn't keep her down for long. She was back in Vietnam in six weeks. I heard one Marine say of her, "There is one brave woman." Second Lieutenant Brown and Leroy were extracted from the battlefield on an Ontos. It felt like we lost a brother and sister in arms!

The other Marine battalions around us were being pounded by the enemy and engaged in heavy fighting. We continued to take incoming mortar and artillery rounds as we kept advancing toward our objective. It was thunderous at times. The noise of their rounds hitting around us and the large volume of our own air strikes and artillery exploding in front of us tested everyone's nerves. It seemed like we were in a turkey shoot, and we were the turkeys. I was talking with Aguon later in the day and he said it best of anyone. "I'd rather face a machine gun than these mortars. At least I'd have a chance to fight back!" Facing machine guns was a deadly proposition but I had to agree with him. At least you could see the enemy behind the gun. Mortars are like death falling from the sky, kind of impersonal if you know what I mean. The number of wounded Marines kept mounting to the point that no one reported their wounds any longer. There were no corpsmen left to report to. The men bandaged themselves and kept moving forward.

The only NVA soldiers we encountered this day were already dead except for one straggler that was quickly exposed of. Thirty-two NVA bodies were found by our forward squads as we advanced closer to the DMZ. Some abandoned weapons and numerous bunkers were found. My men felt the NVA soldiers had enough of us and were content to fight the other units around us. The problem with that thought was they kept inflicting causalities on us. The NVA soldiers destroyed several of our tanks and an Ontos, killing several Marines and wounding several more. We knew they were there but we just couldn't draw them into a fight.

Early that afternoon we stopped and set up a perimeter. Hotel and Foxtrot advanced through us and set up there. Once again, the mortars fell on us. This time nearly thirty rounds hit us around 1850 hours. No place was safe from the mortar and artillery attacks. Finally, the order came down from headquarters to locate the enemy batteries. I am not sure which squad took a forward observer out to locate the enemy position, but they told us that the observer actually climbed a tree in order to see the enemy. They were loading their big guns into trucks to move farther north. Needless to say, they didn't make the move. Our guns zeroed in on them and destroyed their convoy of trucks and guns.

The enemy kept attacking the other units. Hotel Company of 2nd Battalion 9th Marines was suckered into an ambush by the NVA regulars. They were located to our right flank. Several more tanks were destroyed by the NVA sharp-shooters. Hotel took heavy causalities and couldn't advance on the enemy positions. I and the other squad leaders were told, in our debriefing meeting that afternoon, that we were accomplishing our mission. I thought to myself, "At what cost to us?" They also told us that the 3rd Battalion 4th Marines, which had been choppered into a blocking position near the DMZ had not encountered any withdrawing NVA units. That meant they were still near us and had not decided to run. The fight would continue another day. The final result of our meeting was to combine our three platoons into one. The company only had seventy-six Marines left.

We had lost another Marine this day, with forty-five wounded. Thus far we had lost 307 killed or wounded in four days.

✳

Down to One Platoon

Moving to perimeter – May 20

On May 20 our company advanced five hundred meters and set up another perimeter. This time we dug in more efficiently. We stayed on the left flank of 2nd Battalion 9th Marines. Neither they nor we met with any resistance. The NVA soldiers had abandoned their ramparts and moved northwest of us. They ran into the 3rd Battalion 9th Marines that were moving on our western flank and serious fighting broke out between the two opposing forces. Bravery and courage under fire would, again, characterize the day. The NVA isolated Kilo Company of the 3rd Battalion 9th Marines and pinned them down with murderous machine gun and small arms fire. We heard later that a corporal, by the name of Walter Washut, had to take control of the platoon. He was able to link up with the pinned-down company even though they took heavy losses. He lost his life trying to save some of the wounded

Marines. His leadership gave Lima Company enough time to reach their butchered Marines. He was posthumously awarded the Silver Star.

That night two more Marines, Cpl. David Bendorf and Pfc. David Hartsoe, of Lima Company of the 3rd Battalion 9th Marines, held off nearly a company of NVA soldiers trying to ambush the relief efforts of Kilo Company. That is over ninety enemy soldiers. They were killed, but their heroism allowed the wounded Marines to escape their helpless situation. They received the Navy Cross.

The Marines were able to pull back to safety and the area was bombed with heavy airstrikes and artillery. The next day, the NVA soldiers had moved from their positions, and once again they had escaped being annihilated. Twenty-six Marines died and fifty-nine were wounded.

Sgt. Perez – looking for water, May 20

Patrols were sent out from our perimeter in search of water. My squad, and Perez, was one of the patrols looking for water. We found a small stream and filled our canteens, and I must admit it was good to wash my face in that stream. It reminded me of doing the same thing while squirrel hunting back home. My other men enjoyed it, too. We didn't spend long there. We needed to return with the water and the security of the other Marines.

Our company had been reduced in size to one platoon. We were stretched thin. While my squad was looking for water, another patrol of twenty men headed north. It was supposed to be a short patrol but ended up lasting five hours. They found a pistol, holster and a belt with a red star on the buckle. Corporal Mitchell, who was on the patrol with a machine gun team, told me they found rows and rows of reinforced bunkers. They were empty. The NVA had left them. That was a good thing because twenty men would have had a tough fight facing those odds. They also found a bomb shelter near Thon Au Nba. The next day our entire company was ready to move forward.

*

A Needed Rest

On May 21 we were ordered to remain in our positions. Reports from the battlefield came to us and we learned that the 3rd Battalion 9th Marines were still meeting heavy resistance and taking causalities. We always knew when the fighting was continuing because we could hear the sounds of battle in the distance. There was no way we could help them but our blood ran hot wishing we could help. No Marine likes to hear of other Marines in trouble and not being able to help. It is the worst feeling possible. The only good from that day came from watching the A-4's, F-4's and F-8's, from the First Marine Aircraft Wing, drop napalm on the bunkers and terrain in front of our positions. The South Vietnamese Air Force's Douglas A-1 propeller Skyraiders provided close air to ground support. There is never much love between the fly boys and the grunts, but this day we were cheering their every strike. Mitchel loved those Skyraiders. All of us loved the enemy taking some serious damage from their efforts.

*

An Eerie Time

Still under-manned, our platoon rejoined the fight on May 22 and 23. Our company moved into the DMZ along with elements of the 3rd Battalion 4th Marines. We were advancing toward the mountains on the western side of Con Thien. It was very hard going. The brush was thick, and the crossings were treacherous. Many of these gorges had to be crossed on unsubstantial bridges. It takes a lot of guts to make your way across an unstable bridge with one hundred pounds of gear on your back. They didn't appear to be able to hold a small man, let alone all that weight and there was no better place to be ambushed than while crossing a bridge. If we didn't have a bridge to cross it was a fallen tree over a ravine. I never was one to be good at balancing myself while walking on a log. It was frightening.

Ayers resting on log crossing – May 22

Crossing bridge – May 23

The terrain didn't help our confidence, plus the 2nd Battalion 9th Marines had pulled their support from us and moved to the rear. Once again, I drew upon my confidence course exercises and training at boot camp. Believe it or not, the Marines had prepared us for just this kind of situation. I believe all my men felt the same about it!

This was an eerie time for me, and I knew in my mind that we were being watched by the enemy. I can't explain it, but I had a feeling. No enemy had been spotted so I had no reason to have my thoughts. But, they were there. I passed the word back to my men to be on alert. We were especially careful of the paths when we found them. Orders were to stay off of them. Booby traps were a big possibility.

My fears were validated when our CP was attacked. It was a planned attack on the enemy's part. They never assaulted us unless they had the advantage. They used hand grenades and wounded one Marine, and to make things worse, once again one of our own Marines was wounded when friendly artillery rounds fell short of their targets. Plus, several of our men had heat strokes due to the extremely hot conditions.

Our platoon reached what seemed to be an old agricultural develop-ment area west of Con Thien on May 23. We built earthworks there and prepared for whatever the NVA had planned for us. Then, on May 24 Echo and Hotel companies started a sweep of the DMZ. The tanks with us were unable to traverse the terrain so they returned to Con Thien. Our company and Foxtrot moved to the rear of our battalion's advance. Very light contact was made and only a few NVA soldiers were killed until late in the day. Our units came under heavy and savage mortar and artillery attacks from the NVA near Hill 117.

*

Hill 117

May 25 would prove to be another day of severe fighting. Hotel Company was in the point position with their 3rd Platoon on their left flank and the 2nd Platoon on the right flank. Our platoon was in reserve and about three miles to our west flank. Hotel's 3rd squad came under enormous enemy fire as they approached the northern and western slopes of Hill 117 in the early afternoon.

Two of their squads from Hotel Company were fighting at close range with the enemy, so close the muzzle flashes from the enemy mortars could be seen. Their advance up the hill was stopped by the NVA soldiers. The Second Platoon was ordered to assault the center of the enemy position and attempt to make a left turn in an enveloping maneuver to reinforce the pinned-down units but their advance was slowed by stiff NVA resistance. The vegetation was very thick, making the Marines work hard to penetrate the fixed positions of the enemy.

The Marines of Hotel Company bravely represented their unit, but the NVA positions were fortified and the enemy soldiers well-trained.

They allowed the Marines to hack their way halfway up the hill before they opened up on them at extremely close range of no more than fifteen meters. Enemy grenades showered down on the advancing Marines. The assault lasted for one hour with heavy Marine losses. Finally, Hotel Company had to retreat. The Marines have a motto, "no one left behind." Several Marines were killed and wounded trying to carry the wounded back down the hill.

Artillery and airstrikes pounded the hill. Every inch of it was shelled. Company Kilo from the 3rd Battalion 4th Marines joined the fight along with one of our companies, Hotel Company. They charged the hill again at 1345 hours, and met with heavy fire again from the fortified positions farther up the hill. The fighting was fierce and the Marines were at a depressing disadvantage in that they couldn't see the enemy because of the dense brush. It was all they could do to hack through it. They were shooting blind when the order was given to once again retreat. Both companies took heavy losses and had trouble removing their wounded and dead from the hill. The total loss for the day was fourteen Marines killed and ninety wounded.

In the meantime, my squad and the rest of our company were taking stray incoming rounds from the battle in front of us. Occasionally a sniper would shoot at us from the thickets. The order came for us to move closer to the engagement. That movement brought a heavy bombardment of mortars from our flank. One of the rounds landed several feet from my squad. I was hit by shrapnel on the left side of my neck just above my collar bone just missing the main artery in my neck. The piece of metal was so hot it nearly cauterized the wound. The piece of shrapnel jolted my head, and I lost my helmet. I ran to find cover and scooped my helmet up on the way when another mortar hit close to us. I heard the shrapnel buzz over my back. My helmet being knocked off of my head and falling to the ground probably saved me from more injury. Now I had to deal with a sore neck and a sore jaw, but I was thankful to still be alive and in the fight.

Nighttime fell with the NVA soldiers still in control of the Hill 117. Orders came from Col. Masterpool, himself to dig in deep. He was ordering B52's to drop 2000-pound bombs on the hill. He wanted to kill everything living on that hill. The night was one of anxious anticipation on everyone's behalf. My men were worried that we would be called upon, again to take the lead, plus the fear of the B-52's missing their target was gripping everyone's mind. It was a night in which no one slept. The ground shook constantly from the bombing. The B-52's did their job. The next morning found the hill nearly bare of any vegetation, only craters and pieces of standing trees. The hill was covered with fallen trees.

*

Our Forces are Re-Aligned

The next day, May 26, started off with disaster. Lieutenant Colonial Figard was wounded leaving Lt. Col. Masterpool in command, but he and Col. Flathman were wounded in a chopper crash as a result of enemy machine gun fire. They were attempting to evaluate the battlefield from the air. Major Landers took control of our battalion, 2nd Battalion 26th Marines, and Vest took command of the 3rd Battalion 4th Marines. The confusion and re-ordering of the command stopped the planned assault of the hill that day. Instead it was shelled all day by our artillery and airstrikes. The next day, May 27, continued the re-assignment of units. Echo and Foxtrot

Companies of our battalion were assigned to Vest and the 3rd Battalion 4th Marines. That left our company with Landers. The NVA gunners continued to shell our positions with 60-mm mortars. Our unit received over fifty mortar rounds during the day.

*

Hill 117 is Captured

On May 27 Echo and Foxtrot attacked the hill. Our company was too weak to help them this day. Our fighting capability had been reduced to two small platoons. Lieutenant Colonial Duncan Chaplin, III took command. It was a helpless feeling on our part. It was almost like we had failed to come through for them. We were tagged with a nickname when he took command. I don't think we deserved the nickname that was given to us, "Chaplin's Nomads." We were called that name because others were saying we had no home-base. It is true we had moved all around the country since December. But I figured our home was with each other. We were Marines and that means we were a brotherhood. I don't know why it bothered me. I just didn't care for it. I never wrote the nickname on my helmet.

My squad and Mitchell's machine gun team were on Hill 71 on this day. We moved from there around the base of the Hill 117 as Echo led up the hill with Foxtrot behind them. We were looking for snipers. Our Hotel Company had attachments fighting with them. They felt the teeth of the enemy snipers. Later, Mitchell recalled the experience of one of his friends, Royce Ladiner, on that day. Ladiner had three men killed by the sharp shooting NVA snipers. All of them were shot in the head. We had always been told that the North Vietnamese were gutless and untrained fighters. Obviously, that was not true. They knew how to inflict fear in our hearts and they knew how to fight and they earned our respect. Another friend of Mitchell, Joseph Rhinehart, was killed at the same time. He was with Lima Company of the 3rd Battalion 4th Marines. We killed two snipers that day.

The attack was well-planned. Our artillery fired concentrated fire patterns not more than a hundred meters in front of Echo as they moved up the hill. In fact, nearly 1000 rounds fell that day. I cannot describe what it looks like to see and experience that much fire-power landing so close to us, with exploding rounds tossing dirt and tree fragments on our heads. The assault was successful. The main force of the NVA battalion had pulled off the hill and retreated to another location. Echo Company was ordered to slow the advance and the 3rd Battalion 4th Marines moved through them and to the top of the hill. The fight for Hill 117 was over!

*

Hill 174

There seemed to be no relief coming for us. The next day, May 28, we moved our position five hundred meters to the southwest of Con Thien. Even though we were supporting the 3rd Battalion 4th Marines, everyone was dead tired and battle worn. I could see the scars of battle on the faces of the men of my unit. They had endured hell and won, but the toll it took would last forever in their minds and hearts.

Hill 117

The dreaded anticipation of battle was almost too much to endure. We located nearly ninety enemy bunkers and destroyed them. The NVA had abandoned them, but there was another major fight taking place in front of us involving the 3rd Battalion 4th Marines. We could hear the battle. They had backed the NVA into a fight on Hill 174, which would take three days to capture. Our CP was mortared but no one was wounded.

*

The Battle of Hickory Ends

May 29 was a repeat of the day before. We continued to move across the southwestern terrain of the DMZ. The Battle of Hickory, as it would become known, ended at midnight on May 28, but I simply think it changed its name to Operation Prairie IV. However, the killing didn't stop for us. Our battalion, 2nd Battalion 26th Marines, had lost thirty-seven Marines killed and 324 wounded. We killed 207 NVA soldiers. My company, Golf Company, had lost 157 Marines. Only forty had not been hurt in some way. Overall, the fighting units losses were 142 killed and 896 wounded. My battalion had 800 out of a total of about 1000 Marines killed or wounded and the fighting was not over. We had killed 789 NVA soldiers. Nearly 11,000 civilians had been re-located from their homes.

Our orders, for May 29 through May 31 were to patrol in and around Hill 117 and an agricultural center in the area. The higher command figured the NVA would attempt to re-take the high country in the area because of its strategic location. The NVA movement could be easily seen from on top of these surrounding hills. The patrols were uneventful until May 31.

*

The Final Nightmare

May 31 would be another costly day. I will never forget that day. It is burned into my soul. It was the day I was wounded the third time but more important, it was the day I lost a good friend in Cpl. Dennis Johnson. A piece of me died that day. It is not that the other men I fought with were not as important to me. That is not the case at all. I shall never forget Cahalane and his great love for his wife and the lost dreams they both had for the future because of his death. He died on May 24 on a C-130 transport airplane while being evacuated. I will not forget the sacrifice of Sewell, Frye, Manning, Moore, Marshall, Horrell, and Bones. Nor will I forget the devotion Aguon, Cox, Holdgraffer, Powers, Mitchell and Bannister gave to their country and Corps. These men and all the Marines of 2nd Battalion 26th Marines are heroes. Their bravery and sacrifice is ranked in the highest tradition of the United States Marine Corps, but Dennis and I had a special bond.

Dennis was a seasoned Marine by the time I arrived in country. He was the one I counted on so many times that I can't remember them all.

I'll not forget his long and lanky stride or his sheepish smile. He loved the "Mamas and Papas" and especially Mama Cass. I was always kidding him, "Dennis, why Mama Cass? Why not Michelle? She's a beauty!" I was constantly riding him about them but he would come right back at me with, "Hey, Phil, I'm a Californian. What do you expect? Mama grooves." Then he'd do his impression of her shuffling her feet. "They are in my blood!" I think he carried on that way just to stay in touch with back home.

Johnson was from Twain Hartey, California, and he was soon to return there. His time in Vietnam was almost up. He was within days of leaving. We talked about home a lot. "What else was there to do?" His home sounded much like my home back in Virginia. Dennis loved his mountains and spoke of the beauty of the forests and the different seasons. I couldn't believe that California had snow but he swore they would have two and three-foot snow storms. I thought California was all beaches and sunshine. I think that's the reason he sang the lyrics, "All the leaves are brown and the sky is gray. I've been for a walk on a winter's day. I'd be safe and warm if I was in L.A. California dreamin' on such a winter's day."

There was one lake he talked about, Twain Harte Lake. He claimed its beaches were almost of ocean quality. Then, he would laugh. Actually they hardly existed as beaches. His description of home was like listening to a snapshot of Salem, Virginia. Even the radio station, 93.5 AKBN, sounded like my home. He said it was country with a rock twist. Johnson, like many of us, didn't mention our loved ones too much, even though he had a wife back home. It was like it would bring bad luck, especially after Cahalane was killed.

The late afternoon of May 31 found us ascending Hill 173. It was the critical objective in the area because of its height. I thought we were making good time. We were moving at a good pace and a safe one. The enemy was still a real presence in the area, and I wanted to be cautious, but the commanding officers were in a hurry to reach the top, especially our platoon leader, 2nd Lt. Gerst. They ordered the pace to pick up. I had Powers walking point. He was a good Marine and had learned to watch for booby traps and enemy positions, but he wasn't Johnson. Johnson was the best I had at walking point. In my frustration, after receiving orders to pick up the pace, I ordered him to take the lead. I should have never done that to him. He obviously felt the pressure to move faster also. Dennis made a fatal mistake, and tripped a Chicom Claymore mine at 1440 hours. The explosion killed him.

The blast knocked me to the ground and I landed in a thick bush along the side of the trail. I only remember two things. I yelled out, "Oh no. . ." And my eyes were burning like they were on fire. I tried to open them but that made it worse. I couldn't see any clear images. Things were a blur. The corpsman wouldn't give my eyes time to clear and medevac'd me with four other men who were wounded by the blast.

I heard a chopper landing and felt the wind of its blades on my face. I was led to the chopper and strapped into a seat. I heard the Marines loading the other wounded Marines, and I heard them say to be easy with Johnson's body. Their talk stabbed my heart like a knife. I argued to stay but the chopper lifted off and was gone from the hill. It landed in Dong Ha at the field hospital.

Later that day, at 1525 hours, May 31, Pfc. Danny Higgins and Cpl. Everheart were wounded by a grenade booby trap on the same hill. A tank was called to clear the hill of booby traps so several generals could land on top of the hill the next day, June 1. Later a 250-pound bomb was located and blown on Hill 162. Gerst supervised its detonation and was wounded but not evacuated. The generals praised the Marines for their gallantry. I suppose it was a good thing for them to visit. I do know this; it was easy for them to visit after the fighting was over! The battalion would return to Cam Lo in a few days and back to Dong Ha.

The hospital personal helped me off the chopper and took my rifle and gear. I felt naked without it and argued to keep it, but they would have none of that. I wasn't in a good mood. In fact, I was at the point of fighting anyone near me. I was tense and my heart was beating fast. I felt up tight and couldn't even speak clearly. The first thing the medics did was give me IV's. That settled me down. The doctor asked me to open my eyes. He had to pry them open and hold them. The light seemed so bright that it hurt. He asked, "Can you see images?" and I said, "Only black spots." He asked, "But you do see light?" He remarked, "That it was good that I could see light." He asked them to put patches over my eyes and treated them with a salve. He told them to clean the infection out of my other wounds and to stitch them. That wasn't pleasant. They hastily put a splint on my thumb and wrapped my foot. There were to many wounded Marines to be treated to do anymore for me.

Something they said really bothered me, and I have felt guilty ever since I heard the conversation. It is forty-five years later, and I still think about it. I suppose several of the doctors were deciding the extent of my wounds and one questioned if I was faking the eye injury. The doctor who treated me and asked me the questions replied, "No, I don't think so. His face is burned around his eyes and his pupils are not reacting to light. It seems to me he has CS gas burns. I am not, really sure what caused his injury, but he is not faking it." I wanted to scream but I was too exhausted to even defend myself. Sergeant Leith, who was being treated for shrapnel wounds to his foot visited me, and later said I had white phosphorous burns not CS burns, and he feared I might lose my eyesight.

I stayed there for several days and was flown to Da Nang's medical station and, then, back to Dong Ha. Staff Sergeant Perez came to see me and told me I would be going home because of being wounded three times. I disagreed with him over that decision. Several days later I went back to Da Nang and was given the news that I had to leave Vietnam. I had been wounded three times and there was a three-and-out rule. I was angry with their decision. I scolded them and explained that most of the Marines had been hit numerous times and they were staying. "Yes, that is true," they said, "But theirs were not recorded. Yours are and so you have to leave. And besides, you still can't see well enough to go back to combat."

I was flown to Hawaii by the way of the Philippines, where I came under the care of doctors at the Naval Medical Center as an outpatient on June 14. I had to wear dark sunglasses for several months. My vision cleared up over the years even though I have my eyes examined every six months from the results of corneal epithelial damage. My vision worsened from what it was. I no longer had 20/20 vision. Many years later I had surgery on my ankle to correct nerve damage from the war injury.

Ayers in Hawaii

I was assigned to guard duty at West Lock Naval Station. I never saw my men again. I often wonder what they think of me. I stayed in Hawaii until January 1, 1968. I was a bitter person with many issues. I was depressed from being forced out of Vietnam when my friends had to remain behind. I didn't know what to do with my feelings of guilt and my thoughts of my betrayal of them. I was so angry with the world and everyone in it. I saw everyone as my enemy, and I hated it. I was on edge at the time and looking for an excuse to vent. I was a walking time bomb. I was "combat" weary.

Hawaii was not your typical fun-in-the-sun vacation for me. Most Marines would love to have a stay in Hawaii. I liked it, but I had many problems. I was short tempered, as I said, and I isolated myself from others. I went to the beach and just stayed there by myself as much as possible.

I nearly lost my rank over an incident that occurred late one night. A Marine came into the barracks at West Lock where I was assigned duty.

He was coming off of a weekend pass, and was drunk and talking loud. He was threatening with his language and was going to kick everyone's butt. He was acting like a jerk. I took issue with that and promptly challenged him. I was in my sergeant's quarters. I had been promoted to sergeant. I called out to him to settle down. He called me an SOB. That was all it took. Before I realized what I was doing, I had grabbed him by his Adam's apple and was squeezing the life out of him. He was paralyzed in my grip. I saw his face turning white and felt his helpless posture. I turned him loose, and he fell to the floor. I put him into his rack and left him there. He couldn't talk for a week or so. I could have lost my sergeant's rank over it. The only reason I didn't is that, in the investigation, the Marine testified that he was insubordinate and drunk. He said he started the fight and I acted in self-defense. Once again, a Marine stood up for another Marine.

I stayed in Hawaii for seven months. I received orders to go to Camp Lejeune.

18

January 1968
A Sad Return Home

*T*his chapter is devoted to all those war veterans who are having troubles in life. Maybe you still dream about combat, have flashbacks or can't visit funeral homes, or avoid certain sounds and smells. Are you reliving the war, time and time again? Or do you avoid it altogether? Do you cry when taps are played or the National Anthem is sung? Does hearing the Marine Corps Anthem rip your heart out? Perhaps your relationships never work out or are not satisfying to you. You just don't enjoy people any longer. Do you feel guilty, ashamed or depressed over your war experiences? Do you abuse substances? Are you losing control of your anger too often? Are your appetite and sleeping patterns always changing? Do you feel like you are going crazy? Do you worry excessively over your kids, wife and job? Is life just not worth living? Are you overwhelmed by life? Do you think of harming yourself or others from time to time? Then, listen to what I say. I am writing in hopes that you, the reader, will seek help from the Veteran's Psychological Clinic on PTSD. You could *very well be suffering from PTSD. Do not see yourself as a failure or a burden on our government. I did for many years. You are not. There is help for you and you have earned it. Please seek it out!*

*

You Are Not Welcome Here!

I arrived back in the continental United States on January 1, 1968. The public was starting to withdraw their support for the war in Vietnam. This bothered me greatly. So I hope you can understand my dismay and disgust at what I was about to see and hear when I stepped off that airplane at the San Francisco airport.

Coming home should be a rewarding experience, not another reason to hate. I could see large crowds of people from my window seat on the airplane as it taxied up to the gate. They were behind a fence and seemed to be cheering. I thought, "How nice. They have come to greet us." A temporary sense of pride swelled up within me. This particular airplane was full of returning Army, Navy and Marines from Vietnam. Many of them were in casts and used a cane to walk. Some of their bandages were visible. It was obvious they were returning veterans. I thought, maybe this will cheer them up.

The stewardess, a beautiful young woman, announced to us that there was a protest of the war today at the airport and we should try to ignore them once we disembarked the airplane. My happiness turned to more bitterness. I had heard of some of the controversy over the war while in Hawaii, but nothing like this. The people of Hawaii were decent people and loved the military. They were always respectful of us and treated us with dignity. So you can understand why I had a problem with these protesters. It was a surprise to me.

We walked down the long tunnel to the baggage area, picked up our sea bags and headed outside to the street. They were waiting for us with shouting and fist pumping in the air. If there had not been a fence between me and them, I would have showed them something about fists. They were screaming, "Baby killers! Go back from where you came! You are not welcome here!" I didn't say anything, but I was thinking to myself, "You fools, where do think we came from?" My mind wondered to the scenes in Vietnam and the faces of the Marines who had died for these idiots. For a moment I was lost in time. That would happen a lot. I felt myself becoming angrier.

Then it happened. They started to throw eggs across the fence at us. I was not out of range of them so the eggs were landing very close to me. I had to dodge a few of them. Several of the other Marines and a few Navy sailors were walking close to me. The eggs hit several of them. They began to shout back at these people. One sailor picked up a rock which was lying next to a flower garden and hurled it across the fence. I wished it had been a grenade. I wanted them to feel the pain that I and so many of our wounded were feeling. I couldn't believe what happened next.

A police officer came running up to this sailor and arrested him. I asked the cop what exactly was his problem. He motioned for me to back off, but by this time all the returning military men had gathered around the cop, probably thirty or more. Things looked like they were going to get nasty for him. Several other policemen showed up and things became very tense real fast.

The police hand-cuffed the young sailor and attempted to take him to a police car. The rest of us were not going away. There was a lot of shoulder rubbing between them and us. We weren't simply going to move and we refused to step aside. We demanded a reason for this. One cop said, "They have a right to protest. They are legal. They have a permit to be here." A Marine officer demanded to know if they had a right to throw things at us. The cops said they didn't see that happening, only the sailor throwing a rock across the fence at the protesters. We quickly pointed out the eggs lying all over the pavement. Things were really heating up between them and us. I guess these cops figured out we were not going to step aside so easily. What were they going to do, pull their guns on us? The cop doing all the talking had a level head. He decided to rethink the situation, saying, "Take the cuffs off the sailor." So they let the sailor go with a warning.

You should have heard that crowd booing the cops. I thought to myself, "They have a right. . .? What about the rights of those brave men who died for their rights?" Sadly enough, it would only be the tip of the negative press the war was receiving. Somehow, it didn't seem right to me, Marines dying for an ungrateful nation while Vietnamese peasants begged for our help. My friends had paid the ultimate price for their country, and this is their reward. I hate to say it but if I would have had a rifle, I honestly think I would have . . . well, only God knows. The energy had drained out of me. I didn't really see any sense in carrying on. It seemed to me, since I couldn't fight any longer, even the Corps was gone.

I hailed a taxi along with several other Marines, and he took us to Travis Air Force Base, back to where my journey to Vietnam had started. I was not the same person now as I was back then. I had changed, and the change would affect my life for the next forty years. Every decision, every act, every thought was centered on the events of Vietnam, and I didn't realize it! I camouflaged them the same way I camouflaged myself before going on an ambush. I knew something was wrong with me at first but with time I accepted it. My jealousy, my anger, my self-esteem and my personality were controlled by the effects of the war. The pain and depression wouldn't go away. I acted it out for a long time until I started to suppress it into my inner conscious.

I became unapproachable to people and I made sure they kept their distance from me. Sure I had people who thought they were my friends, but in reality they were nothing to me. I didn't know how to love, and worse, I didn't want to know how to love anyone. I figured there was too much hurt lurking there. I developed a philosophy, "I will hurt you first because if given a chance, you will hurt me."

My trip back home took me through Chicago. There was a long layover at the airport so I went inside the terminal to wait for my connecting flight to Roanoke. It was probably me being paranoid but it seemed everyone was watching me as I walked by them. I was proud to wear the Marine Corps uniform, but I will admit that I felt out of place in my own country. I wasn't sure how I was to act or what to say to people who might approach me. It was an awkward and confusing time. I kept to myself and was glad to hear the announcement to board the flight going to Roanoke. I just wanted to get home!

I arrived in Salem on January 7, 1968. There were no parades like there were for the World Wars or Korean veterans returning home. No, everyone was going about their chores as if it were just another day. And in actuality, it was just another day. I was sitting in an isle seat when the stewardess announced we were arriving in Roanoke. I leaned across the man sitting at the window and searched the mountains below us for familiar scenes. The airplane flew in over the Roanoke Star, an age old land mark in the Valley. I was home. My emotions were nearly uncontrollable. I had a sense of relief, like a weight was lifted from me. The gentleman that was sitting with me was an older man. He asked, "Are you back from overseas?" It was his way of asking, "Are you returning from war?" I fought back my emotions and answered simply, "Yes sir." He said, "Welcome back home. I'm glad you made it." I believe he meant it. He will never realize the need I had in my spirit to hear those words. The airplane landed at Woodrum airport. There were no protesters at the gate this time.

I caught a cab to Salem. I didn't comprehend much of the ride to Salem. My thoughts were drawn to Johnson and his family and I wondered what Mrs. Cahalane and the others were doing. I was in deep thought when the cab driver said, "Here you are." Thoughts of these men would consume me for months to come.

The driver didn't charge me a fare when he realized I was a veteran. He had served in Korea and was glad to help me. What a difference from the people in San Francisco. He let me off right in front of Barbara's house. I knocked at the side door just as I had always done, but this time it was different. It seemed strange to me, like I'd never had been there before. Derby answered the door and about passed out. No one was expecting me. I hadn't telephoned anyone. He called out to his mother, "Mom, Phil is here!" I went in the house and greeted Hazel with a long hug. Durwood came into the den to meet me. He was glad to see me. Barbara was out at the time.

We had a grand reunion that evening. Hazel told me about the Marine Corps officers coming to tell Barbara about my being wounded. She said it was the most dreadful thing in her life to open the door to them. She said she thought I had been killed. "Thank God," she said. "You are home! My prayers have been answered."

It was time to see Mike. Durwood drove me to my house on Wildwood Road. "You are unusually quiet today. Is there anything you want to talk about? "No," I replied "I'm just thinking." He drove off. No one was there and the house was empty. Everyone had moved away. I wondered where Mike was living.

I decided to walk to the Brown's home and spent the night there. They, too, were glad to see me. Esther recognized a big change in me right from the beginning. I remember her saying, "You need to go the Veterans Hospital and let them give you a medical examination." I believe she suggested that because she awoke me out of an awful dream that first night I spent with them. It was one of many flashbacks I would live with for a long time. They started immediately after I arrived in Hawaii. I explained to her, "The Navy doctors said it was 'combat fatigue' and would eventually go away." They gave me some sleeping pills to take but they made me so groggy that I quit taking them. Now, the proper name for my condition is Post Traumatic Stress Disorder (PTSD).

My condition ruined my hopes of a life with Barbara. I think I frightened her. And besides, she had met a nice young man and had fallen in love with him. They married and had a beautiful daughter. I drifted away from Hazel and the rest of that family. Hazel never stopped loving me, but I couldn't return the affection. It scared me, so I avoided her. Losing that friendship was the worst mistake I made in life. She loved me like a son, and I was too foolish to understand the value of such a relationship. If only we could turn back the clock. She died before I found help with my illness, but somehow I believe she knows I love her. Barbara best expresses my thoughts: "She will be there in heaven, waiting, and we will all be together. In my mind I can see them waiting!"

I met a woman and we were married not long after I returned home. The marriage produced four wonderful children and lasted eighteen years. They paid a heavy price for my illness. They lived in fear of me. I dictated and forced my desires on them. My anger continually increased and they were the benefactors of it. I was truly sick and I didn't realize it.

My life could be summarized as trying to have everything and do everything in a moment's time. It was as if I would lose everything if I didn't succeed in that endeavor. My life could be described as truly trying to have and do everything in a moment of time. It was like I would lose my chance in life if I didn't have things immediately.

I was miserable. I remember deer hunting one winter. I spotted a buck in an open field, and I waited for it to approach me as if it were a NVA soldier. That deer became one of those individuals. I can't explain it but it was as if I was aiming at a person and not an animal. I slipped back in time and lost sight of reality for a moment. When it was close enough to throw a rock and hit it, I shot it with a very high powered rifle, a Remington 7-mm Magnum Rifle, not one but eight times I shot that deer. I savagely butchered it with shot after shot.

I would walk in the mountains and would find myself back in the mountains of Vietnam in my mind, looking and expecting an enemy ambush. I would shake my head violently trying to kick the memories out of it, but they just came back. Helicopters flying overhead would trigger feelings of hurt, fear and panic. Certain sounds and smells would control my actions and thoughts. Yet, I never put these things together to realize they were symptoms of a sickness stemming from many years earlier. The years passed but the effects of combat did not.

I hated taking orders from my boss on the job, and I was always uneasy around my co-workers. Many times I would argue with them to the point of fighting. I couldn't stand to not finish a job as quickly as I could. Unfinished business haunted me until I completed the work. I was a driven individual.

Eventually people either avoided me or accepted me for who I was. I buried my feelings deeper and deeper into my soul, and my way of living became my down-fall. I hardened my heart more and more toward anything worthwhile to others. I only wanted what I wanted and nothing else mattered to me. But I didn't see this venom in me but it poisoned me to the depths of despair.

Eighteen years passed with me living a miserable life but thinking all my woes were others' fault. Debbie, my oldest teenaged daughter, had prayed for me for a long time and would not give up on me. Her prayers triggered all the old memories of conversations with Mrs. Lamourant, Hazel and Johnson. She continued to push me to attend church with her. God had been on my mind for years, ever since I visited with Rene in South Carolina and my conversations with Hazel. I fought with myself over Johnson and our talk in that church many years ago. Those memories stayed at the forefront of my thoughts, until finally, I agreed to go with her on Wednesday nights to her church.

I had been to church many times since being married. I wasn't opposed to church, but it really had nothing to offer me, how however it was different this time. The Scriptures captured my interest and I started to go on a regular basis. The more I heard the truth about Jesus Christ, the more

I wanted to know. I realized, for the first time, exactly what Hazel was trying to share with me in her kitchen that day long ago. I learned that He died on a cross in my place for the sins I had committed. The Bible said Christ was buried for me and came back from the dead for me so I could be forgiven of my sins. I was hearing all the things that Hazel had talked about a long time ago.

I started to think about death in a different light than before. Death had always been the final chapter for me. But the teacher's presentation of the resurrection of Christ intrigued me, and I found myself embracing the Scripture. Faith was given to me by God and grace flooded my soul. I accepted Jesus Christ as my Savior on March 30, 1980, twelve years and ten months after the Battle of Hickory.

My life took on a different direction. I went to seminary and became a pastor. I thought Christ had healed me of my trauma from Vietnam. I sold my guns and stopped hunting. Very seldom did I think about the war and only on occasion did I have night-mares about it. I really believed I had been delivered from the clutches of war. Actually, I had allowed my faith in Christ to push the events of those former days deeper into my inner-self. My faith was a crutch. I became a minister to help other people deal with their problems, and I ignored mine. I lost myself in others' hurts and pains, yet all the time Christ wanted me to deal with my unsettled wounds. Instead, I buried them.

Then, one weekend in 2008, forty-one years after Vietnam, I went to see the movie, "We Were Soldiers Once." It was about a battle fought by an Army company in Vietnam. All the memories and unresolved feelings that I had hidden in my inner-self came flooding back. I became very emotional. In fact, I believed I was having a nervous breakdown. When I would hear a helicopter flying overhead I would become very emotional. I couldn't hold back the tears, the crying, and the uncontrollable sobbing. No matter how hard I tried I could not push the emotions away. I went to the local veteran's hospital in Roanoke, Virginia, begging for help and I found it. The doctors put me under an ongoing treatment plan. The doctors at the V.A. Medical Center saved my life, and I can't say enough about them. They are caring and wonderful professionals who care about veterans.

I have learned that counseling, medication and the love of Jesus Christ are three powerful elements in the recovery process for me. Part of my instability was not being able to put a time line between the flashbacks. I'd lost everything in-between them. I felt as though I was being dropped in and out of hell. Much of that has changed by facing what happened. I was able to accomplish that by researching the military records and by the help of a few men who were there with me — Billy Mitchell, Bob Brown and Jerry Dallape. I am forever indebted to these men. Again, I have found that Marines help Marines. My emotions and nightmares are manageable. PTSD will never go away but I am productive and life is better!

I still have the horrible nightmares but not as frequently. I dream about Cahalane being hit and the appearance of his legs. I feel the body of that unknown Marine who died in my arms, and I remember his life go out of his body. His eyes I'll never forget. I see the face of Dennis and I live with my choice to send him to the point position that day. I have flashbacks of the close fighting and the faces of the wounded. I see the ponchos with dead Marine bodies lying under them, and I wake up in fear of bullets and mortars hitting me. I smell the garlic and smoldering NVA bodies as if I were still there. I wake up in a cold sweat after reliving diving into that hole with that gook and the blood. And now I have a new picture in my mind. I learned of it while speaking with Mitchell. It is of Frye crying when he saw the boots of Johnson protruding out from under the poncho lying over Johnson's dead body as he walked past him. But in time all these things will pass!

Someone asked me, "How does one keep their sanity?" I answered, "I am learning to live one day at a time, within the grace of Christ!" Love covers a multitude of sins (I Peter 4:8). Jesus is allowing me to heal at a pace that is healthy for me. Many things about my faith and my illness I do not understand; like, why doesn't Christ take it all away? But I believe, "The Lord will deliver me (*and you*) from every work and He will preserve me (*and you*) for His heavenly home (II Timothy 4:18)." Jesus has a plan for our future and it is a great one. He has a purpose for me and you (Jeremiah 29:11-12)! I have a new philosophy now. "If someone must be hurt, let it be me!"

I live everyday with the guilt of having killed other human beings and being forced to forsake my fellow Marines. I am certain that all has been forgiven by Jesus Christ (I John 1:8-9). However, I am learning that I will never forget. The thought of war brings me to tears. But even this pain is moving me to a higher understanding of the mercy and grace of God. Guy Penrod sings, "Saints have a past and sinners have a future!" I believe it.

If you, the reader, have never accepted Jesus Christ as your Lord and Savior, I invite you to do so now. Pray with me, "Dear Heavenly Father, Please have mercy on me. I turn from my unbelieving way of thinking about you. I ask for your help to live a life worthy of your love for me. Grant me your grace, mercy and saving power. I ask Jesus Christ, who is your Son, into my heart to forgive me of my sins and to help me with my faith. I accept the truth that Jesus died in my place on a cross and was buried in the grave and arose on the third day for me. I thank you for loving me unconditionally and for giving me eternal life and a Heavenly home. In Jesus Name I pray. Amen!" (John 3:16; Romans 3:23; Romans 10:8-13and Ephesians 2:1-10)

*

Prayer Moves the Hand of God

I pray that you never forget those who answered the call to go to war. I ask that once you have read this book, that you give a copy of it to a combat veteran. I ask that you pray for our veterans because I have seen the power of prayer in this world. Prayer works! "At your side one thousand people may die, or even ten thousand right beside you, but you will not be hurt (Psalms 91:7)." May God grant to you His grace and mercy for now and forever more!

I have learned there is one relationship that is more powerful and rewarding than that of one Marine to another Marine. It is the relationship a person can have with God's Son, the Lord Jesus Christ. It is through prayer that we can speak with Him. I believe prayer moves the hand of God to bring favor upon His family. To Him belongs all the glory and honor forever and ever. Amen!

Semper Fi!

VITA

Dr. Philip Eugene Ayers

Education:

    A.S., Virginia Western Community College, 1973.

    D.S.Th.., Colonial Baptist College, 1980.

    B.R.ED., Trinity College of the Bible, 1982.

    M.Min., Trinity Theological Seminary, 1984.

    M.A., Liberty University, 1991.

    D.MIN., Liberty Theological Seminary, 2005.

Publications:

    A Proverb a Day Keeps the Devil Away

    ISBN: 978-1-60647-844-8

    What Ever Happened to Respect? America's Loss of Respect

    for Pastors

    ISBN: 1-4208-6623-0 (sc)

    In Jail Once, Imprisoned for Life

ISBN: TXu-1-733-031

Traveling Upward
ISBN: 9781498421836

You may schedule Dr. Phil Ayers for ministry outreach at:

ariseministry.org

or

by mail at Dr. Phil Ayers,

PO Box 364, Cloverdale, VA 24019

philipayers@ariseministry.org

CPSIA information can be obtained
at www.ICGtesting.com
Printed in the USA
BVOW03*1657281117

501474BV00005B/2/P